EDUCATION AS A FORCE
FOR SOCIAL CHANGE

[IV]

FOUNDATIONS OF WALDORF EDUCATION

RUDOLF STEINER

EDUCATION
AS A FORCE FOR
SOCIAL
CHANGE

Translated by
Robert F. Lathe and Nancy Parsons Whittaker

Anthroposophic Press

*The publisher wishes to acknowledge the inspiration
and support of Connie and Robert Dulaney*

❖ ❖ ❖

This book is a translation of *Die Erziehungsfrage als soziale Frage* (GA 296 in the
Collected Works of Rudolf Steiner); lectures 4,5, and 6, the "Volkspädagogik"
lectures in *Geisteswissenschaftliche Behandlung sozialer und pädagogischer Fragen*
(GA 192); and lectures 2 and 11 in *Neugestaltung des sozialen Organismus* (GA
330/331), all published by Rudolf Steiner Verlag, Dornach, Switzerland.

© Copyright Anthroposophic Press, 1997

Published in the United States by Anthroposophic Press
3390 Route 9, Hudson, NY 12534

LIBRARY OF CONGRESS CATALOGING-IN-PUBLICATION DATA

Steiner, Rudolf, 1861–1925.
    [Selections. English. 1997]
    Education as a force for social change / Rudolf Steiner ; translated by Rob-
ert F. Lathe and Nancy Parsons Whittaker.
      p. cm. — (Foundations of Waldorf education ; 4)
    "Translation of Die Erziehungsfrage als soziale Frage (GA 296 in the col-
lected works of Rudolf Steiner); lectures 4, 5, and 6, the 'Volkspädagogik' lectures in Geisteswissenschaftliche Behandlung sozialer und pädagogischer
Fragen (GA 192); lectures 2 and 11 in Neugestaltung des sozialen Organismus (GA 330/331)"—T.p. verso.
    Includes bibliographical references
    ISBN 0-88010-411-2 (pbk.)
    1. Educational sociology. 2. Social change. 3. Education—Social aspects.
I. Title. II. Series.
LC191.2.S74   1997
406.43'2—DC21   97–2781
                                      CIP

10 9 8 7 6 5 4 3 2 1

Printed in the United States of America

CONTENTS

PART I

EDUCATION AS A SOCIAL FORCE

PART II

BACKGROUNDS OF
WALDORF EDUCATION

SYNOPSES OF THE LECTURES

PART I: EDUCATION AS A SOCIAL FORCE

LECTURE 1

Overcoming the present social problems through spiritual cognition. The fundamental difference between the East and the West: considering the external sense-perceptible world as maya in the East and the spirit-soul as ideology in the West. The three-pronged attack upon humanity since the fifteenth century through natural science and machines: mechanization of the spirit, vegetation of the soul, and animalization of the body. Concerning the concept of "social democracy." The historical demand of a threefold social organism: socialism in economics, democracy in justice, and freedom in cultural life. The central question of education. The significance of differing educational principles during the three phases of childhood: 1) imitation until the age of seven is the basis of social freedom; 2) respected authority until the age of fourteen is the basis of a feeling of justice; 3) a general love of humanity after puberty is the basis of fraternity in economics. The fatalistic attitude in peoples' souls in the East and the West. Modern society: a cultural life based upon Greece, a system of justice based upon Rome, and economics based upon European civilization. The threefold social organism as a means of gaining control of the chaotic economic life, of the power struggle in the realm of justice, and of the empty slogans prevalent in cultural life. Lujo Brentano's Law as an example of today's economics. Commodity, Labor, and Capital: understanding these three concepts through Imagination, Inspiration, and Intuition.

LECTURE 2

Echoes of the Greek and Roman soul in the present. The transformation of concepts from the pictorial toward the abstract since the fifteenth century. The strength of concepts is a remnant of prenatal spiritual existence. The task of modern thinking is to comprehend the individual as a spiritual being. The senselessness of the human will in industrial activity. The need to develop sensible willing out of the spirit and an inner feeling of truth at the present time. The transformation of human consciousness exemplified by the differences in perception of Raphael's and Michelangelo's paintings by their contemporaries and by modern people. The limitations of religious consciousness concerning earthly life during the Fourth post-Atlantean period and the necessity of expanding that consciousness today to include the concept of repeated earthly lives. The inner disintegration of people today is a result of deficiencies in education. The need to concentrate on subjects. Economical teaching practice. Class schedules. The tasks of the Waldorf School in Stuttgart.

LECTURE 3

Commodity, Labor, and Capital—three concepts needed to understand social life. Modern economics—practice without theory. Social democracy—theory without practice. The necessity of an imaginative understanding of the world for social life in the future. Imaginative concepts as a precondition for proper socializing. The need to permeate society with: 1) imaginative concepts for a feeling understanding of commodity, 2) inspired concepts for a new understanding of labor, and 3) intuitive concepts for the proper relationship of capital to society. The relationships between Commodity, Labor and Capital. Recognizing the significance of 1) imagination for commodities through fraternity in economics, 2) inspiration for work through equality in justice, and 3) intuition for capital through freedom in cultural life. The significance of rediscovering the connection between work and spirituality.

LECTURE 4

The permeation of pedagogy with a materialistic attitude by modern teacher training. Withering of the soul due to the modern use of illustrative materials in teaching. The need for the teacher to be permeated with an understanding for the relationship of the human being to the spiritual world. The child represents a question from the supersensible world posed to the sense-perceptible world. Anthroposophical anthropology as the basis for education in the future. Inner understanding of the threefold nature of the human being. The head/nerve aspect of the human being. The human chest/rhythmic aspect. The human limb/metabolic aspect. The significance of immortality for the development of the spirit: directing attention toward what is revealed of prenatal life instead of looking only at life after death. Observing the forms of the threefold nature of the human being. The head as a picture of the physical body, the chest as a picture of the etheric body, and the metabolic system as a picture of the astral body. Perceiving the I through observing how humans change in life. Physiognomic pedagogy: Fichte as an example. The present desire to even out the differences between people contrasted with the innermost human desire to be recognized as an individual.

LECTURE 5

The metamorphosis of human intelligence in the course of development. Egypto-Chaldean intelligence as a perception of the relationship of the human being with the cosmos. Greco-Roman intelligence as a recognition of the principles of death. The increasing tendency of intelligence toward evil, illusion, and error. The significance of the Mystery of Golgotha in that connection. The concept of Christ and a general concept of God. Atheism as an illness. The misfortune of not recognizing Christ. The need to permeate Ahrimanically guided intelligence with the concept of Christ. The fear of the incarnating soul to enter into a materialistically oriented world. The melancholic tendency seen in children's faces today. The task of the teacher: to prepare children to find Christ through rebirth. Comprehending the seriousness of our times and the resulting tasks.

LECTURE 6

Concerning the importance of an exact knowledge of human nature. The change of the human physical body from the Egypto-Chaldean plant-like body to the modern death-filled body. Atavistic development of the human body is a cause of tumors. Human physical characteristics in connection with the manner of cognition. The relationship of the human being to the realms of nature in the different post-Atlantean periods. The decline of the human being through animal, plant, and mineral stages. A re-ascension to a knowledge of the living is the task of the current developmental period. The egotism of modern religions: limiting the concept of God to the individual's own Angel. Indifference to the general fate of humanity is an expression of egotistical intelligence. Investigating the goals of human destiny through mediums in the West and mystics in the East. Interest in things extending beyond personal earthly existence is the starting point for understanding the nature of the Archangels. Interest in the effects of the past and the future upon the present is the precondition for forming concepts about the realm of the Time Spirits. Consideration of the impulses in modern cultural, rights, and economic life. The women's movement. Anthroposophic understanding as a guideline for modern activity. The Goetheanum.

PART II: BACKGROUNDS OF WALDORF EDUCATION

PROLETARIAN DEMANDS AND
HOW TO PUT THEM INTO PRACTICE

The need to trust one another. The tasks of the proletariat are different today. The previous assumption that the old German government would continue is no longer valid. The need to look at intent, not just content. The proletariat is harnessed completely by economic life so they can see only economic life. The need to think with a purely human attitude. The need for a complete re-formation, a complete emancipation of cultural life. All cultural work needs to be available to everyone. Relationship of the economic value of work to cultural life. The need to make cultural life, rights life, and economic life independent of one another. Strikes attempt to make political changes through economic activities. The need for liberty in cultural life, equality in the democratic state, and brotherly love in associative economic life.

THE SOCIAL BASIS OF PUBLIC EDUCATION

LECTURE 1

The inadequacy of the natural-scientific worldview to deal with the social problems of the present. The need to renew public schools and the social basis of public education. Criteria for an appropriate pedagogy.

LECTURE 2

Understanding the deeper connections in contemporary history as a foundation for the kind of teaching that touches life. The need to transform teacher training and the nature of examinations.

LECTURE 3

Contemporary methods of education are alienated from life. The teaching of the class periods and its importance for healthy thinking. Renewing art in a way that is connected to life. Its task in the education of the will.

THE TASKS OF SCHOOLS
AND THE THREEFOLD SOCIAL ORGANISM

Teachers must have a voice in how society is reformed. How schools have produced the proletariat. The essence of the proletariat is that their existence hangs in the air. The school depends upon state and economic forces, the teacher is caught between parents and state. Modern people lack inner strength. How to teach to develop the child's thinking, feeling, and willing forces. The socialist program. The demands for democracy and socialism mean that human will must guide all state and economic activity. Children need to learn to be independent. Repetition and authority as the basis of education. Emphasis on thinking, feeling, or willing causes imbalance in the other two. The cultural realm, in particular schools, needs to be independent. The human being unifies the independent cultural, rights, and economic realms. Error in the belief that new is always better. The proletarian child depends upon the content of his or her soul later in life. The child's right to education. Importance of the teacher's personality and talent. Separation of church and state. The teacher's authority. Freedom. Need to make the relationship between governing and governed more social.

TRANSLATOR'S INTRODUCTION

Nancy Parsons Whittaker

For the Western world, the years 1914 to 1918 were cataclysmic. Western society, whether in Europe, England, or America, had collectively marched out of the nineteenth century waving the banners of Science and Prosperity. People widely believed that this wonderful tool, rational science, developed and refined by the best minds on both continents, had placed humanity just steps away from being able to completely eliminate suffering, poverty, and despair.

If you read German, English, and American newspapers and journals from the turn of the century, the dominant message, though couched in the specific culture of each nation, is the same. In Germany, the human intellect, through the objectivity of science, was going to breathe so much wisdom and strength into the political structure of the state that the German people would be able to create an empire that would endure for a thousand years. In England, this same science was going to restructure social relationships so that economic life would be lifted above the vagaries of the marketplace and justice and equality for all would become a reality. In the United States, conventional wisdom held that science was going to eliminate everything that stood in the way of unending progress and prosperity—diseases would be eliminated, engineering and agricultural problems would be solved, and cities would be built or renovated, so that they would shine golden on the horizon.

By 1913, the overriding popular belief within these three nations was that their dearest cultural goals were about to be realized. Germany was building a rock-solid political state to guide the nation far into the future, England was moving toward a society that would ensure economic equilibrium and social justice, and the United States was embarking on an exhilarating path of discovery and achievement, unfettered by everything that had plagued humanity before the Age of Science.

Then came the Great War. From August 1, 1914 to November 11, 1918 volley after volley, battle after battle, drove home the enormity of the error of these beliefs. In England, Germany, and the rest of Europe it was not just the reports of the staggering number of lives lost—*ten million killed*—or the even more incomprehensible number of wounded and maimed—*twenty million crippled*. It was the blackened earth and gutted fields of the countryside, the family homes that lay in rubble, the empty places at the table, the crutches resting in the corner, the guest room that was now the invalid's chamber that tore hope from the human soul and showed the promises of just half a decade before to be but straw in the wind. The German state collapsed completely and English social relationships became confused and uncertain.

The United States would lose 115,000 of its young men in battle. Although it could witness the war an ocean away from the fighting, the numbers of dead and wounded were shocking. More shocking, however, was the emerging picture of the technologies used to wreak such havoc: tanks, planes, machine guns, and, most horrifying of all, poison gas—all made possible by a science thought to be only beneficial. In the United States, this picture of humanity's unwavering friend, revealed as a horrific fiend bent on human destruction, elicited a stunned, shocked uncertainty. Everywhere people numbly tried to piece together a new vision of the future. Progress and prosperity were as uncertain as ever—and possibly not even worth the risk.

There is another story about this war, a true story about foot soldiers in the trenches on Christmas Eve, somewhere on the plains of France. The German soldiers crouched in their trenches against the cold, away from the enemy. The English soldiers did the same. Between them lay the battlefield, where they knew many would draw their last breath on the following day. But that night it was quiet. In the stillness of midnight, an English soldier drew a small musical instrument from his pack and softly began to play "Silent Night." The air was winter-crisp, the sky star-studded, and the solitary notes of one English soldier's song escaped the trenches and filled the battle-field. From the other side, a clear, young tenor joined in with "*Stille Nacht.*" Then, one by one, voices on both sides of the battlefield, in two languages, sang this carol of love in unison. Other carols were exchanged, some known to both armies, others gifts of one side to the other. Afterward, cautiously at first, then in waves of enthusiasm, the soldiers climbed out of their trenches, met each other midway, exchanged chocolates, showed each other pictures of their families and girlfriends, and even struck up a makeshift game of midnight soccer. When the game ended, the first hints of dawn were on the eastern horizon and the soldiers did as soldiers must—they went back to their trenches. The fighting resumed that morning, the war went on. Nothing had changed, except what lived in the hearts of those soldiers and the fact that a small seed of love and understanding had been sown into the life of the Earth.

This story stands in sharp contrast to the raging tides of destruction that the West had loosed upon itself and to the confusion and despair that followed. It is a small story, so small that it appears to be but a pinpoint of light, barely visible on an sea of unending darkness. There is a way of looking at this period of time, however, that brings more than the destructive madness of this war into focus. From this other vantage point, it becomes increasingly clear that this epiphany on the battlefields of France was more than just a wondrous anomaly. It was, in fact, representative of an impulse of much greater significance and truth than anything the Great War brought. Active love was becoming available not just to the hearts of human beings, but to their thoughts and deeds at every level of awareness. This fact has emerged thousands of times, before, during, and after this war. It can be found in stories of groups lifted beyond the desperation of the moment into a place of healing—the Christmas Eve story is only one of dozens documented from the battles of the war itself. It can be found wherever deeply compassionate people devoted their lives to alleviating the suffering of others, and to securing the dignity of all human beings. It is visible in the message and lives of those of the day, who apprehended this impulse most consciously and strove to share it. The soldiers' Christmas, when placed in a truer context, becomes not a solitary pin-point of light, but one of a million stars hung on a velvet canopy, offering both light and direction on the darkest of nights.

Rudolf Steiner was one of those who apprehended this impulse in full awareness and sought to convey it to others. His contributions to the world are unique in that he did not consider it sufficient simply to share his experience and understanding of the highest spiritual realities, though his understanding may have been the clearest and most precise. Beginning in 1917, he worked tirelessly to forge these truths into organizations that could sustain acts of physical, soul, and spiritual healing upon the Earth. There were spiritual leaders of the day who successfully conveyed the concept of universal Love to human thinking, and a few outstanding individuals who were able to breathe it into human feeling. But only a handful ventured into the realm of human will, and no one did so with more vibrant clarity, energy, and strength than Rudolf Steiner. It was his particular gift and task to guide the activity of the highest spiritual truths from sublime thoughts through ennobled feelings, all the way to the spiritualized deeds of those he could find who were capable of such conscious activity. Nowhere was his work more fruitful than in the founding of Independent Waldorf School in Stuttgart.

The cycle of six lectures printed here were presented in Dornach during August, 1919, and can be seen as an act of unification that made it possible, two days later, to lay the spiritual foundations of the Waldorf school. Seen in this light, the form and dynamics of these lectures assume a significance equal to that of their remarkable content. Throughout the first three lectures, Steiner presents again and again the disastrous futility he beheld in the popular political and religious viewpoints of the day—the emptiness, the selfishness, the blindness, the assumptions that, if followed, would tear the human being out of earthly life. To read these sections with an open heart is to enter a realm so oppressive and dark that one feels continually on the verge of losing all bearings. This was the Western world after World War I; this was the numbingly cold midnight experienced by millions of people.

Into the heavy darkness of these first three lectures, Rudolf Steiner weaves one principle: the transformation of the guidance we give to children at various ages. The type of guidance adults provide becomes a living force within the child, which manifests later as adult capacities. The principle he spoke of stood the conventional wisdom of the day on its head, for it arose not from an abstract, logical construct, but from a deep observation and understanding of the interactions of body, soul, and spirit and from an experiential knowledge of the forces of metamorphosis active in all creation.

In brief, Rudolf Steiner stated that, if we wish to educate children so that they are fit to be free adults, we must see to it that, while they are below the age of seven, we offer them an environment where they can intensely imitate the activities of worthy human beings. If we want to prepare children so that, when they are adults, they will experience their fellow human beings as equals, we must ensure that true authorities stand before these children when they are between the ages of seven and fourteen. Finally, Steiner stated that, if we wish our children to become adults who can base their economic, material decisions on the principles of community and human love, while they are teenagers we must teach them with love and direct them constantly to the highest ideals. In other words, if we want the adults of the future to achieve the goals of freedom, equality, and community, while they are children, we must first have them imitate, follow, and revere.

There is nothing in the darkness of the world that makes this principle obvious. What Rudolf Steiner accomplished when he brought this principle forth was to shine a bright, steady beam of light into the seemingly impenetrable darkness of Western society. Once he brought light into the darkness, he was able to pour the most profoundly beautiful spiritual truths into the potential of human activity.

In the final three lectures of this cycle, Steiner's focus is no longer on social forms or even principles of human development. Forms and principles are revealed as mere frameworks, which must be properly filled in order to serve. Once he had established a light in the darkness, what streamed forth was the truth that living, conscious Love, that Christ as Strength, as living motive Impulse, as Principle itself is available to every human being on Earth, and that it is the deepest personal misfortune when we fail to experience the presence of this living, conscious Love in our lives.

. . . .

Not knowing Christ is not an illness, it is a misfortune, a missed opportunity. If you reflect upon the fact that you were born out of nature and out of nature's forces, then, with a healthy soul, you can achieve an understanding of God. If you experience something like a rebirth during your life, then you can achieve an understanding of Christ. Birth leads us to God, rebirth to Christ.... In that rebirth, in finding the spark of Christ in ourselves in an upright and honest ability to say, "Not I, but Christ in me," lies the possibility of not allowing the intellect to fall into deception and evil. That is the higher meaning of salvation in an esoteric Christian sense.... Teachers need to educate children with an awareness that what they are really doing is saving the children, and that they need to bring the children a way of finding Christ as an Impulse in the course of their lives, that is, of finding their own rebirth. (from lecture 5)

. . . .

Here, Steiner implies the deepest goal of what has come to be known as Waldorf education. It may be a child's destiny to experience the rebirth that is the direct apprehension of Christ as Being of the World. Therefore, we must prepare children so that, as adults, they are able to realize such a possibility. The world needs human beings permeated with the Strength, Impulse, and Principle of Love. This education is to be a channel whereby active, conscious love can manifest as the Principle of Life itself.

In these six lectures, Steiner performed spiritually the deed that all schools inspired by his insights must realize in soul and body. He brought light into the darkness of human confusion and then poured reality itself into the space that light had prepared. Throughout his life, Rudolf Steiner added many, many stars to that canopy. All of them heighten our thinking and ennoble our feeling; few of them evoke more responsibility than does this lecture cycle.

CHRONOLOGY OF EVENTS

(leading to the foundation of the First Waldorf School

STUTTGART

December 1916 to September 1919

Of all the myriad events between the December, 1916, German peace initiative and the opening of the first Waldorf school in September, 1919, certain events are particularly important in understanding Rudolf Steiner's original goal of social reformation, and how it transformed into the founding of the Waldorf school in Stuttgart. This metamorphosis in the face of overwhelming historical reality teaches that we must all move toward a greater understanding of truth and set our intentions accordingly.

Nevertheless, spiritual reality will not unite with earthly destiny until we discover what is truly possible, which very often does not resemble our original plans. When Steiner shifted his vision from political and social reform to the creation of a truly human education, he performed such a unification. His life activity itself acts as a healing within the destiny of the modern world.

— Robert Lathe and Nancy Whittaker

DECEMBER, 1916: Germany sends peace note to allies; President Wilson sends peace note to all aggressors.

JANUARY 22, 1917: In a speech, President Wilson replies to the German peace initiative by stating that the basis of a peace must be freedom, democracy, and self-determination.

JANUARY 30, 1917: Steiner characterizes Wilson's proposal as unrealistic.[1]

---

1. See Rudolf Steiner's lecture of January 30, 1917, "The Significance of Spiritual Science for the Present Time," in *The Karma of Untruthfulness*, Part 2 Anthroposophic Press, Hudson, NY, 1992, (GA 174).

FEBRUARY, 1917: Steiner travels to Berlin and remains there until September. Steiner writes the book, *Riddles of the Soul*.[2] He declares that Christ has been perceptible in the etheric world since 1909.[3]

FEBRUARY–MARCH, 1917: The Russian Revolution begins; the United States enters the war.

MARCH 15 AND 17, 1917: Rudolf Steiner describes the relationship between body, soul, and spirit.[4]

APRIL, 1917: Vladimir Lenin travels with other socialists in a sealed train through Germany, reaching Petrograd on April 16 to lead the Bolshevik Revolution in Russia.

MAY, 1917: Otto Graf Lerchenfeld, a member of the Bavarian Royal Cabinet, recognizes the futility of the war and asks Rudolf Steiner for advice.

LATE JUNE, 1917: Steiner begins work with Lerchenfeld to articulate the threefold social organism.[5]

From Lerchenfeld's journal:

Three hours with Dr. Steiner today. The solution to everything lies before me. I *know* that there can be no other. He calls it "threefold social organism" and placed it before me like the egg of Columbus. He wants to work out the details with me in the next few days, but that will probably take weeks.... More than three weeks of daily working for hours followed the first meeting. Weeks of greatest experiences, intensive learning, learning what

---

2. *Riddles of the Soul,* Mercury Press, Spring Valley, NY, 1996.

3. See Rudolf Steiner's lecture of February 6, 1917, "Materialism and Spirituality," in *Cosmic and Human Metamorphoses,* Garber Press, Blauvelt, NY, 1985, (GA 175).

4. These lectures appear as an appendix to *The Foundations of Human Experience,* Anthroposophic Press, Hudson, NY, 1996.

5. The threefold social organism describes an experience of social reality wherein the attributes of the human body, soul, and spirit are seen to exist in human society as the realms of economics, rights, and culture, respectively. Steiner stressed the need for each realm to operate independent of the other two realms, yet at the same time with full awareness and communication. Through full independence assisted by effective interfacing, Steiner saw the possibility of each realm contributing to positive human evolution while effecting social stability and prosperity.

the logic of life means in truth. Learning about growing and dying. Learning how logic must include art so that it is not rejected by genuine life thereby becoming illogic. Politics is an art, not just science and where it is only science, the social organism becomes ill because it is treated as something dead.

JULY 1917: Graft Polzer-Hoditz of Austria joins Lerchenfeld and Steiner in their discussions. Steiner meets with the German ambassador to the United States to present the threefold ideas, but they are rejected. Steiner then prepares memoranda for Polzer-Hoditz to present to the Austrian Minister of Foreign Affairs, who also rejects them.

NOVEMBER 7, 1917: October Revolution; Marxist Bolsheviks under Vladimir Lenin come to power in Russia.

NOVEMBER, 1917: Rudolf Steiner indicates that addressing the problem of evil is *the* task of the present time.[6]

Arthur Graf Polzer-Hoditz discusses the threefold idea with the Austrian Cabinet and prepares a memorandum proposing a process of social reorganization based on the principles of the threefold social organism; it is sent to the Austrian Emperor.

DECEMBER 22, 1917: Peace talks between Germany and Russia begin at Brest-Litovsk where the German Secretary of State Kühlmann does not mention the threefold memorandum (though he has it in his possession).

JANUARY 7, 1917: Hans Kühn requests audience with Prince Max of Baden to present the concepts of the threefold social organism. Prince Max requests the earliest possible meeting with Steiner.

JANUARY 8, 1917: Woodrow Wilson presents his Fourteen Point Program for World Peace.

JANUARY 20 OR 21, 1918: Rudolf and Marie Steiner meet with Prince Max of Baden to discuss the threefold idea. Prince Max, though interested, does not see any possibility of actually using these ideas.

---

6. See Rudolf Steiner's lectures of November 2, 3, and 4, 1917, "The Problem of Faust" in *The Faust Problem*, typed manuscript, GA 273.

FEBRUARY 11, 1918: Wilson presents four points regarding self-determination.

FEBRUARY, 1918: Steiner writes an introduction to an edition of the *Mission of the Folk Souls*, which is presented to Prince Max.[7]

MARCH 3, 1918: Germany demands that Russia sign the peace treaty. Russia signs under protest.

MARCH 21, 1918: The German army begins the Spring Offensive against English forces.

JULY 4, 1918: President Wilson presents further points of his peace program concerning the rule of law and democracy for everyone.

AUGUST 8, 1918: The German army is defeated.

SEPTEMBER 27, 1918: President Wilson presents points concerning justice and equality for all.

OCTOBER 3, 1918: Prince Max becomes the German Chancellor and offers peace to President Wilson based on Wilson's peace program.

END OF OCTOBER, 1918: Germany peacefully becomes a constitutional monarchy.

NOVEMBER 3, 1918: The German fleet at Kiel experiences mutiny, which spreads to Berlin.

NOVEMBER 9, 1918: Karl Liebknecht, leader of the Spartacists, prepared to proclaim a Soviet republic in Germany. Prince Max tries to counter this by proclaiming the abdication of the emperor. Emperor Wilhelm II flees to Holland. The Social Democratic Party proclaims a republic in anticipation of Liebknecht. Prince Max transfers his office to Friedrich Ebert, a Social Democrat. The Social Democrats and the German High Command join unwillingly to create the German republic.

NOVEMBER 7, 1918: Rudolf Steiner begins to work with Carl Unger to form a holding company based on the threefold social organism.

---

7. *The Mission of the Folk Souls,* Garber Press, 1985, GA 121.

NOVEMBER 10, 1918: Workers' and soldiers' councils in Berlin give a revolutionary blessing to Ebert's regime.

NOVEMBER 11, 1918: Armistice between Germany and the Allied forces.

LATE NOVEMBER, 1918: Due to the economic and political collapse of Germany, workers have free time, which Emil Molt attempts to fill with meaningful activity by providing adult education at the Waldorf-Astoria Company.

Emil Molt is approached by one of the workers at the Waldorf-Astoria Company about forming a school for the workers' children.

DECEMBER 19, 1918: Ebert persuades Congress of Soldiers and Workers to fix elections for January 19.

DECEMBER 23, 1918: Revolutionary sailors respond by occupying the chancellery and taking Ebert prisoner.

DECEMBER 24, 1918: Ebert is rescued by troops from Potsdam garrison.

DECEMBER 29, 1918: All three Independent Socialists resign from government to protest Ebert's counterrevolutionary policy.

NOVEMBER, 1918–JANUARY 1919: Steiner spoke extensively about the causes of the war and the need for a new social impulse.

JANUARY 4.1919: Robert Emil Eichhorn, an Independent Socialist and police president is dismissed, leading to mass demonstrations that do not overthrow the government.

JANUARY 11, 1919: Gustav Noske's Majority Socialist (anti-revolutionary) Volunteers enter Berlin and forcibly end the demonstrations. Karl Liebknecht and Rosa Luxemburg (Spartacists) are both arrested and murdered by Volunteer officers.

JANUARY 25-27, 1919: Detailed discussions involving Rudolf Steiner, Emil Molt, Roman Boos, and Hans Kühn result in the decision to write "The Call to the German People and the Civilized World." It is an appeal for honest national reflection and conscious restructuring of social relationships according to the principles of the threefold social organism. This appeal was later signed by a number of notable people from Germany, Austria, and Switzerland, including Hermann Hesse, Emil Molt, Carl Unger, Dr. Lautenschlager (mayor of Stuttgart), Count Otto von Lerchenfeld-Köfering, and Frau Vacano (writer and translator of Vladimir Solovyov). They also decided to establish a school, and to publish Moltke's memoirs as a way to present the causes of the war.

JANUARY 27, 1919: Emil Molt discusses the formation of a school with Steiner, who agrees but emphasizes the necessity that its formation should occur as an independent social action and not as his own creation.

FEBRUARY 3, 1919: Steiner begins to lecture publicly about the threefold social organism.[8]

FEBRUARY 6, 1919: German National Assembly meets in Weimar. Work begins on a new constitution for Germany, the result of which will be the Weimar Republic.

MARCH 5, 1919: "The Call to the German People and the Civilized World" is published in a large number of newspapers in Germany, Austria, and Switzerland. Steiner continues to speak publicly about the spiritual background of social issues.

APRIL 5, 1919: Rudolf Steiner tells Carl Unger that he would be willing to give a course on pedagogy for an independent school.

APRIL 13, 1919: Karl Stockmeyer joins Emil Molt in working on a plan to form an independent school.

APRIL 22, 1919: The Union for the Threefold Order is formed. With the formation of this association, Rudolf Steiner begins a series of lectures over the next three months to workers in various industries primarily in and around Stuttgart.

APRIL 23, 1919: At 11:00 a.m., Steiner speaks to workers at the Waldorf-Astoria Company.[9] Because of that lecture, the workers pass a resolution that they be sent to the government of Württemberg to ask that Steiner be made a member of the cabinet. The intention is that he would work to implement the threefold

---

8. See *Die soziale Frage* (The social question), not translated (GA 328).
9. Contained in the appendix of this volume.

social organism in the state of Württemberg. The resolution was signed by ten to twelve thousand workers of the Stuttgart area.

According to Carl Unger, the resolution was misunderstood, because people thought Steiner wanted to join the present government, something he did not consider, since, in his opinion, if he was called by the government, his first act would be to dissolve the government in its current form.[10]

Following the general meeting at which this resolution was passed, there was a meeting of the Waldorf-Astoria Company Workers' Council, where Molt spoke about his decision to create a school. He had previously spoken with Minister of Culture Heymann, who had promised support for the school. Molt and members of the Workers' Council formally asked Steiner to direct the planned school, and he agreed.[11]

APRIL 25, 1919: Following a lecture at the Daimler Works, Rudolf Steiner meets with Emil Molt, Karl Stockmeyer, and Herbert Hahn for a detailed discussion of the plans and curriculum for the Waldorf school.[12] Karl Stockmeyer is sent throughout Germany to find appropriate teachers.

APRIL 28, 1919: Rudolf Steiner publishes *Towards Social Renewal*.[13]

APRIL 30, 1919: Rudolf Steiner meets with the Minister of Labor to present his ideas of social reorganization. Nothing results.

MAY 11, 18, JUNE 1, 1919: Rudolf Steiner gives a short lecture cycle on public education reform.[14]

MAY 13, 1919: Emil Molt, Karl Stockmeyer, and Rudolf Steiner

---

10. Carl Unger, "Zur Geschichte der Dreigliederung" (Concerning the history of the threefold), in *Dreigliederung des sozialen Organismus* (Threefolding of the social organism), July 11, 1919.

11. Emil Molt, *Von der Gründung der Freien Waldorfschule, August-September, 1919* (On the founding of the Independent Waldorf School, August-September 1919), private publication 1938

12. Contained in *Neugestaltung des sozialen Organismus* (Reforming the social organism) (GA 330).

13. *Towards Social Renewal*, Rudolf Steiner Press 1977 (GA 23).

14. Contained in the appendix to this volume.

meet with Minister of Culture Heymann and his assistant, Reinöhl. Minister Heymann approves the formation of the Independent Waldorf School.

During the middle of 1919, Steiner signs an agreement with Minister Heymann that all children in the Waldorf school will meet the state standards of education at grades 3, 6 and 8; that all their teachers will be personally approved by Minister Heymann; and that the school will remain nonsectarian, while providing denominational religious instruction for those children whose parents desire it.

JULY 31, 1919: Rudolf Steiner concluded his work for a popular movement for social change with a public lecture in Schwenningen: "Socialization and Workers' Councils."[15] Political parties and trade unions absorbed the movement for forming such workers' councils, rendering the formation of independent cultural committees impossible. Steiner was concerned that the movement for a reorganization of society according to the threefold ideas had become too "proletarian."

According to Molt's notes, Steiner remarked: "I have often asked myself what I could have done in order to reach the middle class. First, we attempted to reach the government, but without success. They were merely party members determined to carry out their old programs and had no desire to hear anything new—at least not in the cultural realm. Then we tried to reach the industrialists, also without success. People in those circles simply made fun of what we presented because of our worldviews. Although our first meetings occurred in a purely middle-class context in which people listened to us, our efforts were ultimately ineffective. The basic assumptions of the proletariat were different, however."[16]

AUGUST 9-17, 1919: In Dornach, Steiner presents the lectures contained in this volume.

AUGUST 11, 1919: Weimar Constitution proclaimed. Had it been ratified before May, 1919, the Waldorf school would have been legally impossible.

---

15. There are no written reports of this lecture.
16. Emil Molt in *Die Drei*, August 1925.

AUGUST 20-SEPTEMBER 6, 1919: Steiner gives the basic course on pedagogy in Stuttgart to prepare for the Waldorf school.[17]

AUGUST 31, 1919: Steiner holds a first meeting with the parents of the future students of the Waldorf school.[18]

SEPTEMBER 6, 1919: Following the close of the pedagogical course, Molt and Steiner appoint the teachers for the Waldorf school. Molt discusses salaries with each teacher. "During the first year, the teachers will be employed and paid by the Waldorf-Astoria Company. We had no fixed salary scale, but instead began with the needs of each individual."[19]

SEPTEMBER 7, 1919: Opening ceremony for the Waldorf school was followed by a gathering for the parents, teachers, and children at the school. In the evening, the faculty, the Steiners, and the Molts attend a performance of Mozart's *Magic Flute.*

SEPTEMBER 8, 1919: First faculty meeting with Steiner.

SEPTEMBER 15, 1919: First day at the Waldorf school.

---

17. *The Foundations of Human Experience* (Anthroposophic Press, Hudson, NY, 1996); *Discussions with Teachers* (Anthroposophic Press, Hudson, NY, 1997); *Practical Advice to Teachers* (Rudolf Steiner Press, London, 1976).
18. "Lecture for Prospective Parents," *The Spirit of the Waldorf School,* Anthroposophic Press, Hudson, NY, 1994.
19. Emil Molt, *Von der Gründung der Freien Waldorfschule, August-September, 1919* (On the founding of the Independent Waldorf School, August-September 1919).

PART I

EDUCATION AS

A SOCIAL FORCE

LECTURE ONE

DORNACH / AUGUST 9, 1919

I HAVE JUST COMPLETED a series of lectures and discussions[1] that gave me deep insight into people's current feelings and the tragedy of modern society. Once again, I can return here to Dornach for a few days, to a place so closely connected with the activity we believe can provide the strength to eventually turn the present tragic path of human affairs in a more positive direction.

Perhaps in no other period has there been less inclination to raise people's souls to the spiritual worlds, in the truest sense, than there is today. Nonetheless, it is especially necessary to do that now. The strength people need to proceed along the path of human development can come only from the spiritual worlds. A wide range of people believe we can solve the problems presently confronting us through thoughts and ideas arising from a material perspective. It is difficult to say how long it will be before enough people become convinced that only upon the spiritual path can we find a real solution. Thinking about this question is not very fruitful, but it is certainly clear that we can move forward only when enough people become convinced that the solution to those problems comes only from the spiritual world.

Modern people are greatly concerned with social questions, but they are ill-equipped to think about them because the intellectual capacities of a large part of society are practically paralyzed. Most people believe we can overcome the present social problems with our current knowledge and understanding. We will not overcome them, we cannot overcome them, if we do not tackle them from a spiritual point of view.

We have just gone through a long war. A prolonged struggle will probably continue. Many people say that the war we have experienced is the most terrible event since the beginning of recorded history. We cannot claim this conclusion is false. However, the ensuing battle I refer to will be a war between East and West, between Asia, Europe and America. It will in all likelihood be the greatest spiritual battle humanity will ever undertake. Everything that Christian inspiration and determination have brought to humanity will crash down onto civilization as great primal waves of destruction.

Today, we can state the great divergence between East and West in a simple formula, but that formula is not so simple as it appears. It encompasses a tremendous expanse of human views. You will recall that in my book *Towards Social Renewal* I drew attention to the fact that for a large segment of modern humanity spiritual life is only an ideology. They see everything contained in modern civilization—law, ethics, science, art, religion, and so forth—as nothing more than a wisp of smoke rising above the one and only true reality of economics and material production. I spoke of this when I was here several months ago.

Ideology—that is the response you receive from many modern people when you speak of spiritual life. In truth, though, ideology is everything mirrored in human souls of "the one and only reality," economic reality. There are many reasons we should think about the modern meaning of the word "ideology." It means a great deal. We cannot make a closer connection between that word and any other than its connection to the word from Oriental wisdom, "maya." "Maya," "illusion," translated properly for Western understanding means "ideology." Every other translation is less exact. Thus, a large number of Westerners express the same basic concept or idea with the word "ideology" that an Oriental expresses with the word "maya." But what a tremendous difference! What does the Oriental think of as maya? The Oriental thinks everything in the sense perceptible world is maya, everything perceived by our senses and all thinking connected with sense perceptions is maya, the great illusion. The only reality is the reality of the soul. What a human being achieves in his or her soul is reality. What arises and blossoms in inner life is reality. What presents itself to the senses is maya, illusion, ideology.

Conversely, a large number of Westerners are convinced that the only reality is the reality perceptible to the normal senses. For them, reality is exactly what the Oriental calls maya. On the other hand, Oriental reality, namely, what arises and blossoms in the soul, is for a large part of Occidentals only maya, ideology. You can see the discrepancy. Oriental reality is called ideology in Europe and America, and Western ideology is called reality in the Orient.

Those viewpoints eat into people's souls and form two distinct kinds of beings. If you look at recent events in the civilized world, you will recognize that everything said about the causes and motives of the world catastrophe is simply superficial. The primal forces characterizing that terrible battle arose from the unconscious depths of the human soul. Today, we can see that people do not even know why they took part in it. The reason lies in the elemental forces brought to the surface by divergent views that are far from being resolved. The present antisocial force is so strong that humanity is now divided into two essentially different kinds of people.

If you consider all I have said in this regard when you look toward the West, you will see an aspiration toward freedom. Whether people there fully understand freedom is not so important, the tendency is toward freedom. The desire for freedom stirs in the dark recesses of the human soul.

Now look toward the East. Everything the West calls freedom has no real meaning in the East. There, people have no comprehension of freedom; they cannot connect any feelings with it. People think the least about those things they experience most intensely. Just think how little attention they give to everyday natural occurrences. People do not think about their most immediate experiences. The Oriental living in the view of reality prevalent there, namely, inner reality, lives in freedom to the extent possible within his or her racial, national, or tribal context. The Oriental gives no thought to this. However, the more westward we look, the more we see that freedom has been lost in the course of historical human development. There, people long for freedom because they do not have it.

I could give many more examples of the fundamentally different views of East and West. There are already some indications of what the next few years may bring. The modern events in Asia that are kept secret in Europe for well-known reasons are simply symptoms. The spiritual perspective of the Indian people gives them a very different picture of the fact that half the population is starving from the one that arises here in Europe under similar external circumstances. Humanity is divided into two essentially different groups even regarding such external events. Hunger means something quite different for the Indian than it does for a European because Europeans and Indians have thousands of years of different soul development behind them. People who want to understand the course of human development must look closely at such things. We need to be aware that the problems facing society are much more complicated than people commonly believe. Today's social problems are simply a side effect of the cultural development that began in the mid-fifteenth century. I have often mentioned the important turning point in human history that occurred in the mid-fifteenth century when the modern coloring of science and industrialism began. Modern science and industrialism are the expressions of the forces that entered human development and gave modern human spiritual development its particular direction.

I have often spoken about the nature of science[2] and about how intelligent people[3] view it. People who think about science realize it does not give a true picture of the world but only a shadow of it. Everything that scientists have thought up and that people consider common knowledge, more common than many believe, is a belief or, more properly, a superstition about a phantom world. Then this combines with the spiritual effects of modern industrialism. However, we should look more closely at the spiritual significance of industrialism. Take, for example, that embodiment of industrialism, the machine. Machines differ from everything else people encounter in normal life, such as animals. You can apply all your scientific or other thoughts to an animal —I do not want to even begin talking about human beings in this respect—and regardless of how much you examine it, it still retains an aspect of something we might call a "creature of God." You can never completely discover the essence of an animal. There is always something hidden in the idea of an animal. That is not less the case for plants or even crystals. If you take all the wonderful crystal forms, you have to admit that even though, with some training, you can comprehend crystal forms and so forth, there are still many aspects of crystals you can look at in awe and cannot comprehend simply with conventional intellect.

But now look at a machine—it is perfectly transparent. You know everything about it: we apply power here, the bearings are here and there, the amount of friction is so and so much. Thus, you can calculate its efficiency if you know all the factors involved. There is nothing about a machine we cannot understand with normal intelligence and reasoning. However, that is significant for the relationship of humans to machines. If you have met thousands and thousands of people who work with machines, then you will have learned what the souls of such people have slowly absorbed. You will see, or perhaps only sense, what has crept into people's souls from these spiritually transparent machines. What makes machines so devastating for people is their spiritual transparency: all the forces and interactions in machines are so clear and transparent to the human mind. Mechanical clarity draws life out of the human heart and soul, makes people dry and inhuman.[4]

The combination of science and machines threatens civilization with three forms of destruction if we do not pull ourselves together enough to look toward the supersensible. The scientific ideal, namely, to model everything after the astronomical picture, is slowly gaining the upper hand. The ideal for many people is to model all our understanding of nature after the astronomer's model of the universe. Think about how chemists picture molecules. They imagine molecules as composed of atoms connected to one another by certain forces, so that the result is like small planetary systems. The ideal is to explain the whole world astronomically, but the goal of astronomy is to view the structure of the universe as a machine. Add to that all the work people do with machines!

Those are the things that have had an increasingly strong effect since the mid-fifteenth century and are now robbing human beings of their humanity. If people carry the thinking of mechanistic astronomy and industry into the remainder of life, then their spirits will become mechanized, their souls sleepy and vegetized, and their bodies animalized.

Look at America, the epitome of mechanized spirit. Look to the eastern part of Europe and Russia; the urges and instincts roaming wild there are terrible, and they result in the animalization of the body. In the middle, in Europe, we find sleepiness in the soul. Mechanization of the spirit, vegetation of the soul, animalization of the body—that is what we must face without delusion.

The way we lost the third element of life along with the other two is characteristic of the path of human development since the mid-fifteenth century. A powerful modern political party calls itself the Social Democrats, thus welding socialism and democracy together, although they are the opposites of each other. They were welded together, but the spiritual was left out because socialism relates only to the economic realm and democracy relates only to the rights realm, while the spiritual relates to individualism. The name "social democracy" omits freedom, otherwise it would be called individual, or individualized, social democracy. In that case, we would express all three human desires in one such slogan. It is characteristic of modern times that we omit this third aspect, and that the spirit, in a certain sense, really becomes maya, the great illusion of civilized western humanity, that is, of Europe and its colonial descendants in America. This is where we must begin when we consider spiritual science as a major cultural question. Actually, we cannot even discuss current demands, since they are historical demands. Socialism is a historical demand, and we can properly understand it only in that sense. Democracy is a historical demand. However, liberalism, freedom, individualism are also historical demands, but modern people seldom notice them as such. It is not possible to discuss the situation further unless we recognize the social organism in its three aspects: socialism in economic life, democracy in the life of rights, and freedom or individuality in cultural life.

That is, in truth, the only salvation for humanity. Although those are the intense and unyielding historical tendencies of the present, we should not delude ourselves into thinking that no other demands will appear to those who have a deep insight into the situation. Adults need to live in a society that is economically social, governmentally democratic, and culturally free.

The main question for the future is how we will conduct ourselves with children if we want to raise them to be, in the broadest sense of the words, social, democratic, and free adults. One of the most important problems for the future, a problem already confronting us, is the question of education. Anthroposophy has already pointed to how we should understand education at the present time if we want to move forward. The demands of society will remain chaotic if we do not see that the reason for this chaos lies in the urgent question of contemporary education. If you are interested in the general outline of the education question, you need only look at my book *The Education of the Child in the Light of Anthroposophy*.[5] There I have brought one of the most important problems in modern society to the surface, namely, social education. An understanding of the three periods of child development as presented by spiritual science needs to be more widespread.

You know that in the period between birth and the age of seven, which concludes with the change of teeth, human beings are imitative, that is, they do what they observe in their surroundings. If you look at young children with some understanding, you will always find that they are imitative and do what "big people" do. For young children, it is extremely important that the people around them do only what they should imitate. It is important that you think and feel only what children should imitate when you are in their presence.

Children carry their prenatal experiences in the spiritual world into physical existence after birth. In the spiritual world, we human beings live in the beings of the higher hierarchies; everything we do arises out of the nature of the higher hierarchies. There, we are imitative to a much greater extent because we are united with those beings we imitate. Then we are placed into the physical world, but we continue our habit of being at one with our surroundings. The habit of being at one with the beings in our surroundings, of imitating them, continues. We continue to imitate those who are responsible for our upbringing and who are to do and feel only what we should imitate. It is extremely healthy for children to be able to live not so much in their own souls, but in the souls of the people around them.

In the past, people could rely upon the instinct to imitate because their lives were more instinctive, but in the future, this will no longer be possible. In the future, we must attend to the fact that the child's behavior is imitative. In raising children, we need to continuously keep in mind how we can best create the most favorable environment for their imitative behavior. Everything done in the past regarding imitation must become more and more conscious and more and more consciously connected with the future. People will need to remind themselves that if children are to grow up to meet the needs of the social organism, they must be free. People become free only if they were intensively imitative as children. We need to intensely develop the strength, the natural strength, of children in preparation for that time when they begin to become socially interactive. In spite of all political complaining about freedom, and in spite of all the other talk, people will become free only if we ingrain the strength of imitation in them during childhood. Only what we thus implant during childhood can serve as a basis for social freedom.

You also know that from the age of seven until puberty, that is, until the age of fourteen or fifteen, children have a strength we could call "acting upon authority." Children experience a great uplifting if they can do everything because a person they look up to says it is the right thing to do. There is nothing worse for children than attempting to develop their judgment too early, before puberty. Children's sense of authority will need to be more intensively and more highly developed between the ages of seven and fourteen in the future than it was in the past. We must, with increasing consciousness, direct all upbringing and education during these years toward awakening in children a pure and beautiful feeling toward authority. What we implant during these years will form the basis for what adults within the social organism experience as equal rights for their fellow human beings. A feeling for equal rights for other human beings cannot exist in adults if a feeling for authority is not implanted in them during childhood. Otherwise, adults will never become mature enough to recognize the rights of others. It may well be that in the past a much lesser degree of feeling for authority was sufficient. However, in the future, that will no longer suffice. We must strongly implant in children this feeling toward authority so that as adults they will become mature enough for what arises as a historical demand and is not open to argument.

We should arrange everything in elementary education so that children achieve that perspective during this stage of development. Now, I ask you not only how far modern people are from an insight into such things, but also how far is modern teacher training from such insight? How must we work to make that insight known? It must become known because only through it can we find healing.

If you travel today to countries where the first revolution has already occurred, what do you find in their policies for so-called unified schools? What are their policies, actually? For those who have insight into the connections within human nature, the socialist educational policies are truly shocking, they are the worst imaginable. The worst possible things you could think of are the schools and lesson plans and school organization connected with Lunatscharsky,[6] the minister of education in Russia. What is playing out in Russia as an educational policy is the death of all real social thinking. There arc also socialist educational policies in other parts of Europe that are truly cancerous because they are based upon an absolutely unbelievable idea, the idea that we should organize schools in approximately the same way that adults should live within society. I have read such policies whose first statement is that we should eliminate the principal's office, that teachers and students should be absolutely equal and that we should base the entire school upon an attitude of comradeship. If you say anything against such ideas, for instance, in southern Germany where things have progressed much less than in other areas of Europe, then you are looked upon as someone who has absolutely no understanding of social life.

However, those who have honest intentions regarding the progress of humanity toward a truly social society must be clear that such a society can never develop through socialist educational programs. If we introduce socialism in thc schools, a social attitude cannot exist in life. People can mature enough for socially responsible community life only if they learn to build their lives upon that true authority they experience during their school years. Today, we must make it clear how far people's actions and imagined needs are from what we should be doing and what truly relates to reality.

After puberty, from the age of fourteen to twenty-one, more than sexually oriented love develops in people. That form of love is only a special form of a general love of humanity. The strength that arises from a general love of humanity needs particular care at the time when children leave elementary school and go on either to higher education or into an apprenticeship. The feeling of fraternity, that is, a general love of humanity, can never warm the relationships in economic life as history requires if we do not develop a love of humanity during these years.

The kind of fraternity we must strive for in future economic life can exist in human souls only if we form education after the age of fifteen so that we work completely consciously toward a general love of humanity, and only when all questions regarding world views and all education following the unified school are based upon a love of humanity or, more generally speaking, a love of the external world.

We must base what should bloom within future humanity upon these three aspects of education. If we do not recognize that the physical aspect of the human being is imitative and needs to imitate proper things, we will only implant animalistic urges into the human physical body. If we do not recognize that from the age of seven until fourteen, the etheric aspect of the human being needs particular care and must be developed upon authority, then we will only develop a cultural sleepiness in human beings, and the strength necessary for justice will not exist.

If we do not recognize that, beginning at the age of fourteen or fifteen, we need to bring the power of love connected with the astral body into all teaching in a reasonable way, then children will never develop their astral bodies because they will be unable to form them into a free aspect of human nature.

These things are completely interwoven, and thus I must say: imitation in the proper manner develops freedom; authority, justice; and fraternity or love, economic life.

However, the reverse is also true. If we do not develop love in the proper manner, freedom is missing, and if we do not develop imitation properly, then animalistic urges prevail.

When you look at the problem and consider the major historical trends, you can see that spiritual science is the proper foundation for our present goals and for the future content of culture. Without the proper cultural content, which we can derive only from spiritual science, humanity will not be able to truly develop further.

Therefore, we must bring the problems before us into a spiritual context, and that must become the conviction lying within human souls. I need to emphasize again that we can discuss how long it will take for such a conviction to permeate people's souls, but it is clear that people cannot reach what they strive toward unconsciously without this conviction. From this, I believe you can see the connection between our work in the specific areas of spiritual science and what has resulted from modern needs, from great historical trends and human necessities for the present and near future. That is also why I have often said that we need to consider spiritual science in connection with great modern tasks. Today, though, people are very, very far from being able to judge things in the way I have characterized them. People need a kind of stress, a kind of dissatisfaction to counter their purely material tendency and motivate them to change direction toward spirituality. Otherwise, how will people find their way toward understanding the great question of our time along a path contrary to the path prepared by maya and ideology?

What has actually happened? The impulses that arise in human souls from Eastern or Western thinking are quite different when seen concretely. There is, however, something curious about this, namely, that these impulses create the same mood of soul in both East and West. We would do well to look at this mood more closely. The Oriental view that the external world is maya is old. It was an important mystical understanding of the world in earlier times, but it is no longer true. A kind of passive subjugation has entered this Oriental view precisely because it is outdated. This fatalistic attitude spilled over into Europe in the crassest manner through the Turkish culture. Fatalism—let happen what will—means passivity of the human will.

The Western view of maya exists in the way the West lives in an atmosphere of fatalism.

Marx and Engels, whose view is the modern socialist principle, most precisely expressed that viewpoint of ideology—a viewpoint in which everything connected with the spirit and soul, which is maya, an illusion, arises only from the one single reality, namely, the economic process.

How did this appear in the world? Fatalistically. Until the catastrophe of the World War, what was the external expression of the socialist principle? It was the concentration of capital. Larger and larger capitalists or capitalistic groups formed, trusts, monopolies, and so forth. The economic process progresses through its own momentum, capital concentrates more and more in the hands of capitalist groups until the time arrives where the ownership of capital goes to the proletariat of its own accord. People need to do nothing at all because it is an objective, purely economic process, thus fatalistic.

The Orient arrived at a point of fatalism, but the Occident began there, at least for a majority of the population. The majority of the population is fatalistic. The principle of the East became one of allowing everything that occurs in the world to happen to you, but that is the starting principle in the West. Fatalistically allowing everything to occur is a cultural principle in the East, but in the West it is a material economic process. People everywhere look at the development of human society one-sidedly. If you have an overview of current developments in human society and how they arose from earlier situations, you will find a spiritual element that has become ideology. What is its basis? It is based upon Greek culture. The deepest tendency in the makeup of our souls contains something that is fundamentally Greek. This is why we have the classical preparatory schools (*Gymnasien*) that are an educational imitation of the Greek soul. In Ancient Greece it was natural for people nearing puberty to be so disposed, because the Ancient Greek culture developed in such a way that the majority of people were either Helots[7] or slaves. Their conquerors were of a different bloodline and were the bearers of spiritual life, the rightful bearers of spiritual life. Greek sculpture expresses that particularly well. Look at a bust of Mercury with his ears, eyes, and nose placed quite differently (I have often mentioned this[8]). Through the characteristics the Greeks sculpted into Mercury, they hinted at the people they had conquered, at those people to whom they left commerce. The Aryan, characterized in busts of Zeus or Hera or Athena, was the one upon whom cosmic powers bestowed the spirit.

You should not believe that what manifested as the Greeks' soul structure expressed itself only in their general soul constitution. The way words are formed in the Greek language, a language based upon a socially aristocratic soul, also expresses it. We still have this in our culture, which means that we did not experience a renewal of culture in the mid-fifteenth century, but only a renaissance or a reformation, a kind or refreshing of our cultural life. This all still exists in our own culture.

We teach the students in our classical schools in a manner foreign to life. It was natural to teach youth in Ancient Greece the way that our youth are taught in classical schools because that was the Greek life. The Greeks raised their children and youth according to their own way of life, but we raise our youth according to the way of Greek life. For this reason, our cultural life has become unreal, foreign, and is perceived as an ideology. Our culture is incapable of understanding life and incapable of grappling with and being active in life.

In addition to these cultural aspects, we have also undergone a remarkable development regarding rights. We can find the major change in human development that occurred in the mid-fifteenth century in all areas of life. Grain and everything made from grain is too expensive today. It is overpriced! If you search for the time when it was too cheap in Europe, you find that this was in about the ninth or tenth century. Then, it was just as much too cheap as it is today too expensive; and in the mid-fifteenth century it had a fair price.

It is interesting to see how the major change that occurred in the mid-fifteenth century played right into the price of grain. What happened when grain prices were fair for the greater part of Europe? In about the middle of the fifteenth century, serfdom began to disappear. Then, Roman law forced its way in to destroy the beginnings of freedom. Just as the Greek spirit and soul permeates us, the Roman concept of law also permeates our politics and government. Until now, we have been unable to create anything more in the area of rights than a renaissance of Roman law. In our social organism, we have Greek cultural forms and Roman state structures.

In economics, a renaissance is not possible. Of course, we can live according to Roman law and educate children according to the Greek spirit, but we cannot eat what the Greeks ate because we would never satisfy our hunger. Economic life must exist in the present. Thus, we have European economic life as the third element. We must create order in these three chaotically mixed areas, and we can do this only through the threefold social organism.

People like Marx and Engels saw things very one-sidedly when they recognized we can no longer model our society after the Greek ideal and can no longer govern according to Roman law. They concluded that the only thing remaining is economics, but they considered only economics. As Engels says, we

may only administer commodities and guide production processes, we may no longer govern human beings.[9] This is just as
one-sided as it is correct—correct, but terribly one-sided.

We must set economic life upon its own basis. Within the
economy of the social organism, we must administer commodities and guide production processes. That must become independent. However, if we remove the former basis of rights and
culture from the social organism, then we must establish a new
foundation. That means that alongside economic life, which
administers commodities and guides production processes, we
need a democratic government based upon equality among
human beings. We do not need just a renaissance of Roman
law, we need a new birth of the state based upon the equality of
human beings. We do not need just a renaissance of culture as
occurred at the beginning of the modern era, we need a new
formation, a new creation, of culture. We must become aware
that we are standing before the task of re-creating cultural life.

There is a connection between what lives deep in the development of modern humanity and what the threefold social
organism expresses. It is not a sudden idea, but something born
out of the deepest needs of our times, something particularly
appropriate to the present. There are people, many people,
who say they do not understand that; it is too difficult. In Germany, when people repeated how difficult this is to understand, I told them that these things are to be understood
differently than people have become accustomed to understanding things in the last four or five years. During that time
people found it easy to understand things I did not understand, since they only needed someone to order them to understand. All people needed was an order from headquarters, or
some other authority, and they understood things because they
were ordered to understand them. People even framed these
orders. Now, however, it is important that we understand

things with a free human soul, but to do this, our souls must awaken, something they have little desire to do. But that is what is important. It is not that things are difficult to understand, it is that we lack the will and courage to look at reality. It is quite natural that we must say those things we need to say to humanity in a new tone, in sentences different from those to which people have become accustomed. It is natural because we are caught up in three things quite different from those spoken of in the threefold social organism.

There, a renewal of cultural life is necessary for people to really perceive the connection of their souls with objective spiritual life. People do not have that now. When people speak today, to a large extent they speak in slogans. But why do they speak in slogans? That can only be because they have no connection with the meaning of those slogans. People no longer have a connection with spiritual life, so their words have become slogans.

Much has been said in recent years about maintaining human rights, at least in the civilized world. Events of the present provide sufficient evidence about how far people are from reality concerning rights. People have spoken about rights, but they actually have no concern for justice, only for power.

Likewise, people have not had thoughts capable of encompassing economics and therefore it has gotten out of control. Economics has been characterized simply as more and more production. That is what I said in Vienna in the spring of 1914[10] when I remarked that this continuous production is a cancer in society. More and more was produced, the products were thrown onto the market, and the whole economic cycle continued on by itself without any thoughtful control. Chaotic, unplanned economics, rights that are only a struggle for power, culture debased to slogans: these are the three basic aspects of our present-day society. We must escape from them, but we can escape only if we earnestly try to understand the intent of the threefold social organism.

As you can see, this relates to an understanding possible only through spiritual science. Something I said a few weeks ago in a public lecture resulted in much consternation; however, it is a basic and factual point. Then I said that our present leaders may no longer rely upon their brains, which have become decadent. They must rise to a comprehension of things that no longer requires the brain, but instead uses the etheric body. The thoughts brought together in Anthroposophy do not require the brain. Because of their physiological development, our leaders and members of the modern bourgeois class must accustom themselves to acquiescing on matters of spiritual knowledge while taking care of what can be taken care of with decadent brains.

The proletariat still have fresh brains and move forward. The lemon is not yet squeezed dry; an atavistic characteristic of the brain still exists. That is why the proletariat understand what is said today about a new social structure. The situation today is such that essentially all the proletariat, except their leaders, are open to these things. Their leaders have become middle class; they have become the most narrow-minded of all. They have taken over the realm of middle-class narrow-mindedness and developed it to a high degree. On the other hand, though, within the proletariat there exists a terrible penchant for obedience, and this submissiveness must be broken before there can be any improvement.

Things are now more complicated than people usually think. Essentially, only the science of initiation can provide the means that lead to a correct understanding of modern social problems. In my book *Towards Social Renewal*, which I wrote not only for Anthroposophists but for the general public, you will find three important concepts mentioned concerning modern social life. The first is the economic concept of commodity or products. Another important concept is that of labor, and the third is the concept of capital. An understanding of the modern social situation depends upon these three concepts.

Think of everything social science has said to explain these three concepts. If you know what was said in economics in the second half of the nineteenth century to explain the concepts of commodity, labor, and capital, then you are aware of all the useless scientific work that resulted from an incomplete science of economics. I recently mentioned the example of the famous professor Lujo Brentano,[11] a leading modern economist in Middle Europe who recently wrote an article entitled "The Industrialist."[12] In it he develops three characteristics of an industrialist. I will mention only Brentano's third characteristic, namely, that industrialists use the means of production at their own cost and risk. It's true, isn't it? Industrialists own the means of production and undertake market production at their own cost and risk. Now, the concept as formulated by Brentano, that leading light of modern academic economics, is such that in the same article he deduces whom, along with an industrialist, we may also call an entrepreneur, namely, the worker. The modern worker is also an entrepreneur because he also has means of production, namely, his ability to work, and offers these on the market at his own cost and risk. Brentano's concept of an entrepreneur is so clear that workers also fall into this category. You can see how clever modern economists are. The situation is ridiculous, but today we are unable to laugh about this because the universities have the position of leadership in cultural life. However, universities produce this sort of thing in the field of economics. People will not admit, nor do they have the courage to admit, that such ridiculous work is produced. Things are simply terrible.

We absolutely must look at these things and ask, how is it possible, particularly concerning the burning questions of the day, that science cannot shed light on these social concepts? I would very much like to discuss this question with you during my visit here; but, today I can only touch upon why this is so.

As simple as the economic concept of commodity is, you can never fully comprehend it by normal science. You can never completely understand the concept of commodity if you do not begin with an imaginative understanding. You cannot comprehend the concept of labor, socially or economically, if you do not base your understanding in inspiration. You cannot define capital if you do not bring in intuitive understanding.

The concept of commodities requires Imagination;
The concept of labor requires Inspiration;
The concept of capital requires Intuition.

If these concepts are not formulated in this way, only confusion results.

You can see why only confusion results if you look at a particular case. Why does Brentano so closely connect the concept of capital with the concept of entrepreneur that the worker then becomes a capitalist, or entrepreneur? He is, of course, a very wise man of the times, but he has absolutely no idea how to use intuitive cognition to obtain a true concept of capital.

Of course, this all comes about indirectly. The Bible gives some indication of this path when it speaks of capitalism as mammonism[13] and thus connects capital to a particular kind of spirituality. However, we can only understand spirituality through intuition, and if we want to understand the spirituality active in capitalism, namely, mammonism, we need intuition. That is what the Bible contains, but today we need an understanding of the world appropriate to modern times.

We must attempt to understand objectively these things we hold to be somewhat twisted today. Genuinely objective knowledge in these areas will show the necessity of permeating social viewpoints everywhere with true spiritual science. This is what unprejudiced modern observers of life must impress upon themselves. Perhaps you recall a question posed to me some time ago following a lecture in Basel. During the discussion, someone asked how we could make Lenin ruler of the world. According to that person, the world situation would not improve until Lenin became the ruler of the world. Imagine the kind of confusion this indicates. What this means is that those people who present themselves as the most radical are, in actuality, the most reactionary. They want socialism, but we need to begin by socializing the ruling relationships. However, those people begin socialization with a universal economic monarchy led by Lenin. They do not even begin to socialize the relationships between the governed and the governing. That is how grotesque things are today. It is certainly something to think about when you are told that Lenin should become king of the world, but that is how things are today. Those who believe they have the most progressive concepts have, in actuality, the most twisted ones. People will not come to any clarity in this area if they cannot admit that we must seek such clarity through spiritual science.

LECTURE TWO

IF YOU WANT TO UNDERSTAND the task of Anthroposophy in the present and in the near future, then you must consider the nature of human development since the middle of the fifteenth century, as we did some time ago and then again yesterday. In the end, everything that occurs in the present depends upon the motive that has lived within humanity since the middle of the fifteenth century. Since that time, human beings have been driven to become complete personalities by placing their individuality in the foreground. In the earlier post-Atlantean developmental periods, this was not possible, nor was it the task of humanity. If you want to understand the significance of that change of direction in which we now stand, then you must look at things in more detail than I did yesterday.

In our cultural life, our souls still have a Greek attitude. The manner in which we form our thoughts, the way we customarily think about the world, is actually an echo of the Greek soul. The customary manner of looking at rights and everything connected with them is an echo of the Roman soul. In our government, we still see a structure that is basically that of the Roman Empire. Only when we can see that the threefold social organism must break in upon our modern chaos will we be able to understand clearly and act decisively.

We can characterize the Greek soul primarily as the attitude predominant in Greece and in historical development until the middle of the fifteenth century. A subjugated people and their conquerors lived throughout the Greek territories. The conquerors occupied the land and, through their bloodline, determined the spirituality of Ancient Greece. You can, therefore, never fully comprehend the attitude of the Ancient Greeks if you do not recognize that then people saw the social interactions that resulted from the peculiarities of the Aryan conquerors' blood as proper. Of course, modern humanity has grown beyond what was basic for the Greeks. For them, it was obvious that there were two kinds of people, namely, people who worshipped Mercury and people who worshipped Zeus. These two classes of people were strictly separated. However, everyone thought about the world and their gods in the way that the conquerors, due to their blood characteristics, did of necessity. Everything resulted from the clash of the conquered and conqueror. If you look more closely at what lives in people in our modern society, you will see that those things living in our feelings and subconsciously in our souls no longer accept that aristocratic view of the world. However, the aristocratic worldview still lives in our ideas and concepts, particularly if we have been educated at one of the secondary schools. The higher schools, in particular the classical high schools, educate so that everything is only a renaissance or echo of Ancient Greek culture. With the exception of the technical and agricultural colleges, this is even more true of our institutions of higher education. Technical and agricultural colleges arose out of modern life, but unfortunately they were patterned after higher education in Ancient Greece, at least in their outer structure. If you highly value the culture of Ancient Greece in its time and for its time, you must be clear that a renewal of cultural life is necessary now. You must recognize how increasingly intolerable it is to have humanity led by people whose souls have received their configuration of concepts through our modern classical education. In all leading positions today we find only people who have been educated in our modern classical secondary schools. We need to recognize that a time of major change, not of minor reformation, is at hand, and we must think about such things objectively and not cling to our own habitual thoughts.

You know, of course, that what formed from the blood in Ancient Greece became abstract in Ancient Rome. I have already mentioned that. Although the Greek social structure—we cannot call it a government—arose strictly from bloodlines, this did not continue with the Romans. In Rome, the desire for the Greek organization continued, but the Romans no longer felt the basis of this organization in the blood. It would never have occurred to the Ancient Greeks to doubt that there were lesser people, the conquered, and higher people, the Aryans. That was no longer true for the Romans. In the Roman Empire, people carried a strong consciousness that power and force determined the division of society. You need only recall that the Romans traced their origins back to that band of thieves called together to found Rome. You know that the founders of Rome were not nursed by their mother, but by a wolf in the forest.

All these things were integrated into the Roman nature and resulted in the Romans dividing society more according to abstract concepts. Thus, our legal and governmental concepts resulted from the Roman disposition.

In this connection, I'm often reminded of an old friend. I met him when he was already quite old. In his youth, at the age of eighteen, he fell in love with a girl and they became secretly engaged. But neither of them had any money, so they could not marry. They waited and remained true to one another. He was eighteen years old at the time he became engaged, and before he could consider marrying he was sixty-four. Only then had he saved enough money to believe he could dare take such a step. He went back to his hometown near Salzburg and wanted to marry the one he chose so long ago. When he arrived, he saw that the church and rectory had burned, and he could no longer obtain his baptismal certificate. His baptism was no longer registered, so no one believed he had actually been born. I remember quite well when his letter came. At that time, I lived near Vienna. In his letter he told me, "I think it is quite evident that I was born, because here I am. But people do not believe that I was born because I don't have a baptism certificate!"

I once had a discussion with a lawyer who told me that in a legal proceeding, it is not at all important whether the person is present or not; all that is necessary is the birth certificate.

You never forget such stories because they are so absurd. Nevertheless, the ideas these stories exemplify show that the basis of our entire public and legal life to a greater or lesser extent is what existed in Ancient Rome. How true it is that today you are not a citizen of the world simply because you are a human being and exist, but because you are properly registered. We can trace all such things back to Ancient Rome. Blood lineage changed into official registration.

Today, these things are degenerating, with the result that many people believe they have no value as human beings, but only have the value of the official position they hold or of this or that official designation. People would rather be an impersonal Roman legal concept than an individual personality. Since the middle of the fifteenth century an unconscious or subconscious desire has existed to center everything around the individual. We can see this in the fact that the time is ripe for a renewal of both our cultural and our rights life, and that we need a true renewal. This is connected with the need for a renewal of human souls and with many tendencies lying deep within human development.

Consider how the scientific way of thinking, particularly when based upon abstract natural laws and sense perception and upon the thoughts created from that perception, has affected the cognitive aspect of human development since the middle of the fifteenth century. People accept nothing except what arises out of sense perception and the thoughts connected with it. I reminded you yesterday that there are certainly enough modern people who hold the correct opinion, namely, that such a view of nature leads us only to a phantom picture of nature. The picture of the world created by natural scientists is a phantom and not the real world. Since the middle of the fifteenth century, humanity is capable of making a phantom picture of the world, at least regarding half of it. For initiation science, something is hidden deep behind this that we must now consider.

We cannot change our sense perceptions, and it is basically unimportant for a deeper view of the world whether we see them as maya or as something else. We cannot change sense perceptions, they are what they are. A red flower is a red flower, regardless of whether we view it as maya or as reality. It is what it is. All sense perceptions are what they are. The real discussion begins only when we create thoughts about sense perceptions, that is, when we view sense perceptions as being this or that, or interpret them as this or that. That is where the difficulties begin. Why do they begin there? They begin there because the concepts that we as human beings have created since the fifteenth century are different from earlier human concepts. Modern history is actually a *fable convenue*, a convenient story, and does not correctly consider that at all. Those who have had an opportunity to study human concepts before the middle of the fifteenth century know that those concepts were filled with a pictorial quality, that they were actually living pictures. The abstract quality of concepts has been present in its current form only since the middle of the fifteenth century.

Why has humanity developed such that since the middle of the fifteenth century we have abstract concepts, concepts we are so proud of and are so emotional about? Why do we, humanity as a whole, develop such abstract concepts? The abstract concepts created by humanity have the peculiarity that, although we apply them to the sense-perceptible world, they are not really applicable there. They are worthless for the sense-perceptible world. I spoke about this in my book *The Riddles of Philosophy*.[1] There I said that the way people create cognitive concepts about the outer world is a side effect of human soul development. Imagine a seed of grain in the earth that is predestined by nature to become a plant. We grind many grain seeds to make flour and then eat them as bread. However, that is not inherent in the grain seed! It is unrelated to the nature of grain if we ask whether the grain contains those chemical elements we need to maintain our bodies. It is not in the nature or essence of grains of wheat or rye to feed us, but only to produce new wheat or rye plants. In the same way, it does not lie in our nature to grasp the outer world through those concepts we have learned since the middle of the fifteenth century. Rather we need to learn something else from those concepts if we are to enter properly into their true nature. The concepts people have developed since the middle of the fifteenth century are shadows of our experiences in the spiritual worlds before conception. Allow me to draw this so that you can better picture it. [Rudolf Steiner now draws and describes.] Here is birth, and human life goes in this direction. When you imagine it that way, our concepts and power to conceptualize are only echoes of our experiences before birth. We misuse our conceptual capacity when we apply it to the sense perceptible world.

Birth

(red)

That is the foundation of the Goethean understanding of nature. Goethe did not want to express natural laws through concepts. He wanted to understand archetypal phenomena, that is, he wanted a synthesis of external perceptions because he had a feeling that we cannot directly apply our ability to create concepts to nature. We must develop our ability to form concepts as pure thinking. If we do that, they point toward our prenatal spiritual existence. We have our modern way of thinking to reach, through pure thinking, our spiritual essence as it existed before we were clothed with a physical body. The real task of the Fifth post-Atlantean period will not have entered human souls until humanity comprehends that we think in order to comprehend ourselves as spiritual beings. In a certain sense, natural science was forced into human fate so we would remain with pure nature. That is, so that we would not speculate about it, but use our conceptual thinking to see nature in the proper way. We need to develop our conceptual thinking to see how we were spiritually before we were clothed with a physical body at birth. Today people believe they should use their conceptual thinking simply to classify external sense perceptions. They will act correctly, though, only when they apply the thoughts they have had since the middle of the fifteenth century to the spiritual world where they were before they were clothed with a physical body.

That is how people of the Fifth post-Atlantean period are forced toward the spiritual and prenatal life. Through yet another thing, people come into a peculiar situation that they must develop further. Parallel to the natural scientific phantom is that of industrialism. I mentioned this yesterday. A major characteristic of industrialism is that machines, the actual bearers of industrialism, are spiritually transparent; there is nothing in them we cannot comprehend. Yesterday, I mentioned that even minerals preserve something that is not transparent, but machines are perfectly transparent. The result is that when we direct human will toward machines, we do not, in truth, direct it toward reality. The machine is basically a chimera of comprehensive world reality. Industrialism brings something into human life that makes the will meaningless in a higher sense. A major change will occur when modern people finally become completely convinced that the machine and everything connected with it and with industrialism makes human will meaningless. Today, we are at the peak of mechanical efficiency. Machine power, not human will, now produces a quarter of everything made on Earth. A quarter of everything! That is something extraordinary. Human will no longer has a reason for living on Earth.

When you read things like the speeches by Rabindranath Tagore,[2] you must actually feel something in them that remains unintelligible for a European using normal European intellect and reasoning. A different basic tone exists in the things a modern educated Asian says because the European spirit's accustomed familiarity with the machine is something unintelligible and senseless for an educated Asian. The effects of machinery and industrialism are meaningless to an Oriental. Another thing is just as senseless to an Oriental, whether we in Europe believe it or not, and that is the European politics of the machine age. The Oriental can make no sense of that, either. When educated Orientals speak, they express their feeling that a quarter of all human work now done is senseless. (People educated in the traditional Oriental manner do not do this, only those more directed toward the West and their imitators, the

Japanese and so forth.) Since modern educated Orientals have a higher degree of atavistic clairvoyance, they recognize that everything people put into machines as work has a very particular characteristic. When someone plows the field with a horse and plow, working with the horse, the work with the horse still contains some natural forces and some significance beyond the present; that work has a universal significance. When a wasp builds a nest, this structure has cosmic meaning. If someone starts a fire by striking flint against a stone, causing sparks to fly that then ignite the tinder, that person exists in unity with nature, and the act has cosmic significance. We have lost our connection to cosmic purpose through modern industrialism. There is no universal consequence when we turn on an electric light. Cosmic meaning is gone. When you go into a modern factory completely filled with machines, what you find is a cosmic hole, something without consequence in cosmic development. If you go into the forest to gather wood, that has some cosmic importance beyond earthly development. If you look at a modern factory with everything it contains, that has no importance beyond earthly development. Human will is misplaced there and has no universal purpose. Think about what that means. Since the middle of the fifteenth century, we have developed a cognition that is fantastic, distant from reality. We direct more and more of our activity toward serving machines; we carry out more and more of our activity within industry, and the will we put into this industrial activity is meaningless for cosmic evolution.

A great question now confronts our souls: Does the fact that our knowledge is, to a large extent, fantastic and our will meaningless have any significance for the totality of human development? Yes, it has significance, extremely important significance. It means that as human beings we must forge our way past that fantasy into an understanding of reality, into that understanding of reality that does not stop with nature, but continues on into the spiritual existing beyond nature. As long as people received the spirit along with their concepts, they could neglect to exert themselves to gain the spirit. However, since now only concepts remain, concepts devoid of the spirit, but people still want to reach up to the spirit, many people long to rise above abstract understanding and gain real spiritual understanding. Since we now have industrialism and its lack of meaning, we must seek another meaning for the human will. We can seek that meaning only when we rise to a worldview capable of bringing meaning to what is meaningless, namely, to industrialism. We can do that by bringing meaning from the spiritual and recognizing that we are to seek tasks set for us by the spiritual. Earlier, if we wanted something from the spiritual, we did not need to exert ourselves, because instinct connected the spiritual with human will. Today, we must especially exert ourselves to will out of the spirit. We must counter meaningless industrial willing with a meaningful willing out of the spirit.

Yesterday, I gave you an example of how we should teach. We need to understand that until the age of seven, children are primarily imitators because they need to develop their physical bodies. Thus, we should make imitation the primary principle of education during that time. We also know that from the age of seven to fourteen children need to develop their etheric bodies through a respected authority, and we should make the knowledge we gain through spiritual cognition the basis of our teaching during that period. Finally, we know that from the age of fourteen to twenty-one, children's astral bodies develop, so we should use that knowledge as the basis of our teaching. Only then can we will out of the spirit.

Until the middle of the fifteenth century, people instinctively willed out of the spirit. In external life, we now will completely to integrate ourselves with the mechanical, with machines. Even in politics, our willing toward the mechanical has slowly made the state into a machine. We need to make an effort toward a spiritually founded willing based upon an acceptance of the idea of spiritual science. For example, in education we should begin with an understanding of the spiritual world and teach according to the knowledge we gain from Anthroposophy. Through a stronger and more conscious emphasis of spiritual willing, we counter the meaningless willing arising from industrialism.

We are given industrialism, with all the monotony it brings to human beings and human souls, so that we can use that boredom to work toward willing arising from the spirit. In education, we can best begin to will from the spirit if we teach in a manner consistent with what spiritual understanding requires. We must rethink many things today, but to do this, we need a carefully developed inner sense of truth. We should be clear that we need to use an inner sense of truth even though we are unaccustomed to using it. For instance, you would quite astonish many people if you were to say that they were correct in honoring Raphael[3] because of his paintings, but that they would be mistaken in demanding that modern people paint as Raphael did. The only people who have a right to admire Raphael are those who know that only a poor painter would paint in the same manner today, because this would not be painting out of the impulses active in our time. People's feelings are not consistent with the times if they do not deeply feel the need for that consistency. In our time, we need to have an intimate feeling of truth about this way of seeing things. However, modern people tend to go more in the opposite direction in this connection. You slowly gain an impression that this sense of truth has sprung a leak, that it no longer functions properly because people shy away from calling what is right, right and what is wrong, wrong. They are afraid to call a lie a lie. We experience all kinds of horrible things in this regard, and worse still, people are oblivious to all the terrible things they experience. The point here is that people need to have such a sense for the truth that they know, for example, that Raphael's style of painting does not belong in the present. We need to view it as something from the past, and, thus, also to admire it as something from the past. Now we particularly need to pay attention to such things when a desire for truth overcomes us out of the depths of our souls. I often think of a beautiful passage in Herman Grimm's biography of Michelangelo where Grimm discusses Michelangelo's *Last Judgment*. Where he speaks about how many Last Judgment paintings were made in those times, he also mentions that the people of that time completely experienced the reality of what was painted on the wall. Those people lived in the truth of those paintings of the Last Judgment. Today, we shouldn't even look at a picture like Michelangelo's *Last Judgment* without being conscious that we do not perceive it in the same way as the people for whom Michelangelo painted it. We should be aware that we have lost that feeling, and that at best we can say it is a painting of something we can no longer directly believe to be reality.

Think about someone standing before that painting with today's consciousness, someone who does not think that angels really come down, or that the devil does what Michelangelo depicted in his painting. Such a person views that painting much differently than someone in Michelangelo's time who saw those pictures as reality. However, just when you become aware that the feelings modern people have when they view *The Last Judgment* are something abstract and gray, you will be inwardly called upon to empathize with the interwoven pictures within *The Last Judgment*. Of course, Michelangelo painted during the ebb of the Fourth post-Atlantean period. Nevertheless, he painted out of the spirit of that period and stands as a kind of boundary between both. I once discussed that in a lecture on art.[4] You will need to ask yourself how it was that people of that age could look upon such powerful living pictures presented in paintings. The tremendous importance of that question confronts us when we become aware of how drab and lacking in life are the feelings of someone standing before such a picture by Michelangelo today. We must then ask about the cause. Why is it that human souls of that time could see the end of the Earth in that way? Where did the composition of these pictures come from?

The answer lies in the following. During the first Christian period, that is, since the time the Mystery of Golgotha took effect upon the Earth's evolution and gave it meaning, much that existed of the old ways had to recede and wait for humanity to later win them back. Among those things was the idea of repeated earthly lives. If we depict life [Rudolf Steiner draws here], all human life flows in this manner: Earthly life, life in the spiritual world, earthly life, life in the spiritual world, and so forth.

The content of the ancient atavistic, instinctive view of the world was that the entirety of human life flowed in this manner. The first task of Christianity was to arouse human concepts other than those of ancient wisdom. How did Christianity achieve this? It brought human life into consciousness only from this point forward [see cross in the drawing], that is, from the beginning of the present earthly life. It allowed life before the last death and before birth to be only a thought held by God, not anything connected with human individuality. Before the human being actually became a human being at birth, there existed only the spiritual world, out of which human beings arose as God's thoughts. Then life after death was added. In a sense, during the first Christian period, the focus shifted: Here, life between death and rebirth, then earthly life, then, again, life between death and rebirth, and so forth. Human perception was limited to looking only toward human origins and then toward life after death. On the other hand, this resulted in a counterbalance through paintings of the Last Judgment. Paintings of the Last Judgment arose because Christianity first eliminated the principle of pre-existence from human feeling, that is, spiritual existence before conception and birth. Today, the need to recognize repeated earthly lives once again flows from the depths of human souls. For this reason, today those paintings pale that emphasize only one earthly life and the spiritual world before and after it. An intense desire now exists to expand the Christian view of the world from that of earlier times. The Mystery of Golgotha affects not only those who assume *one* earthly life, but is also valid for those who know of repeated earthly lives. We need this expansion now. We should be aware that we live in a time where we should use the chimera of normal conceptualization, the meaninglessness of mechanized willing, to raise ourselves toward spirit cognition and a spiritually permeated willing, and to expand our religious awareness to include repeated earthly lives.

People now need to take the full import of this present expansion of human consciousness deep into their souls. The ability to understand how to live in the present and to properly prepare for the future depends upon this. Everyone can use that understanding wherever they may now be in life. Eventually, there will arise out of an external understanding of the human being something that presently only plays in the subconscious depths of the soul but that will later sound and resound with the weight of full consciousness. The most obvious thing in modern life is the many torn human souls, troubled souls who know nothing about how to do anything with life, asking time and again, "What should I do? What is the meaning of life for me?" They attempt so many things and still are never satisfied. The number of people with such problematic natures increases more and more. Why is that? It arises out of a deficiency in our education. Today, we educate children in a way that does not awaken the inner strength that makes human beings fit for life. What makes people strong is that they imitate until the age of seven and follow admired authority until the age of fourteen. What makes people strong is that their love is developed in the proper manner until the age of twenty-one. Later, that strength can no longer be developed. What gives people troubled natures is that the forces we must develop in particular stages during youth are not awakened. That is what we must know!

That is why I said yesterday that if we want to have a truly social future, we must prepare for that through education. We cannot achieve that through small changes, the necessary changes are great. Our way of educating has slowly become something that prepares only mechanized spirits, vegetized souls, and animalized bodies, as I described yesterday.

We may not continue in that direction. We should strongly develop the forces existing in children's souls so that, later, human beings can draw upon their childhood development. Today, people look back upon childhood, they feel their childhood, but cannot draw anything out of it simply because nothing was developed. We must fundamentally change our principles of education if we are to have any hope of achieving what is right in this question. Right now, we must be very skeptical when people enthusiastically promote things, when things are touted as being particularly helpful.

Children need to learn to concentrate, and we can achieve that, not through overwork, but through efficient teaching. We can achieve that in the way modern people need if we eliminate something that is very popular today, namely, these cursed class schedules, the death of any genuine development of human strength. Think about what that means: from seven to eight, arithmetic, from eight to nine, language, from nine to ten, geography, ten to eleven, history! Everything that moved the soul from seven until eight is erased by what happens from eight until nine, and so forth. We need to get to the bottom of the problem. We may no longer consider subjects simply as "subjects." Instead, we must see that we properly develop thinking, feeling, and willing in children between the ages of seven and fourteen. Geography, arithmetic, and so forth should all be used to develop the proper manner of thinking, feeling, and willing.

There is much talk among modern educators about how we should develop individual capacities and how we should discover from the child's nature which capacities to develop. Just empty words! Such things can have meaning only when spoken from the standpoint of spiritual science, otherwise they remain just empty talk. In the future, we will need to say that, for instance, at a particular stage of childhood we should teach arithmetic. During that time, we should use the mornings for two or three months to teach arithmetic. We do not need a class schedule that mixes everything together. Rather, we need to teach arithmetic for a time and then go on. We need to bring our teaching into harmony with the needs of human nature at a particular time.

Here you can see the tasks of a pedagogy working toward the future. In such questions, incontestable problems confront modern people earnestly considering future social development. However, there is little understanding for them. In Stuttgart, in connection with our social activities, we will create a school to the extent possible within the modern school system.[5] Mr. Molt[6] has decided to form such a school for the children of his workers at the Waldorf-Astoria Company. Later, we will also admit a limited number of other children. We will need to take into account the teaching goals now set by the state. We will need to bring the children to a certain level by a particular grade, and we will also need to make compromises. However, we can mix those things demanded by human nature with those things demanded by the state, those clever things so idolized by today's socialists. That is a fact that we must all recognize. Who today would think that the class schedule is the death of all genuine human education? There are people who believe in these class schedules to whom we would reply that the world is standing on its head, and we must begin to set it on its feet. There are people who now want to shorten the hours and teach a different subject every half-hour, one after the other. Many people now consider that to be an ideal. You should just imagine what an impossible kaleidoscopic picture that would present—religion, arithmetic, geography, drawing, singing! It would look just like the colors in a kaleidoscope, all mixed up in the children's heads. It "looks like something" only for the external world, but there is not the slightest coherence. Modern people simply do not believe that we need to think in broad strokes instead of details, that we need a grand overview, a comprehensive overview. Today, we experience time and again that people habitually say, "Yes, we must have a revolution!" Even a large portion of narrow-minded conformists believe in the need for revolution. I am not certain if that is the case here, but there are certainly large areas where a majority of the middle class believes in the necessity of revolution. When, however, you approach them with things that I speak of in *Towards Social Renewal*, such as the threefold social organism, they say that they do not understand it, it is too complicated. Lichtenberg[7] once said that when a head collides with a book and makes a hollow sound, it is not necessarily the book's fault. It's true, isn't it? Today, people don't believe such things because there is not always a self-recognition of what is most commonly found in people's souls. Nevertheless, we can see that in many areas, even the reactionaries believe in the need for revolution. But, then they say, "Yeah, yeah, we can't be concerned with such big things and such thoughts. What you need to tell us is how to socialize shoemaking, or how to socialize the pharmacy, how we can do that. You ought to tell us how to sell our spices in a revolutionary state."

Slowly you begin to realize what people mean by that. They mean that there must be a revolution, they are in complete agreement with that, but everything should remain as it is and nothing should be changed. Many people are asking how we can turn everything topsy-turvy and yet not change anything! The people who are most remarkable in this connection are the so-called intellectuals. You can have very strange experiences with them. One thing I have often experienced is that they say, "Yes, three social realms—an autonomous university because cultural life should be self-administered—but how are we to live? Who will pay our salaries if the state no longer does?"

We need to look at these things now. We may no longer simply brush them off. Change is especially necessary in the area of cultural life.

LECTURE THREE

MY REMARKS TODAY will be a kind of interlude. As I mentioned, I want to speak briefly about three concepts that, if people completely understood them, could give rise to an understanding of external social life. I expressly say "external social life," since these three ideas derive entirely from human communal activity and work. These are the concepts of Commodity, Labor, and Capital. I have previously mentioned that various shades of recent economic theory have attempted to clarify those concepts, but have failed. Since the time people began to think consciously about economics, clarity has not been possible. Before the beginning of the Fifth post-Atlantean period, that is, before the period beginning in the middle of the fifteenth century, people could not consciously comprehend social relationships. Social relationships proceeded more or less unconsciously, or instinctively. Since then, however, because this is the period for the development of the consciousness soul, people need to think more and more consciously about social relationships. For this reason, people have developed all kinds of ideas and viewpoints about society. First, there was the mercantilist school, then came the physiocrats[1] Adam Smith,[2] the various Utopian streams, Proudhon,[3] Fourier,[4] and so forth, right up to the modern Social Democrats on the one side and conventional economic theory on the other. It is interesting to compare Social Democratic theory, based upon the work of Marx, Engels, and others, with conventional economics. Conventional economic theory is totally unproductive. It contributes absolutely nothing in the way of concepts that people can integrate into social willing. If you ask what you should do for society, you will gain nothing from the twisted and chaotic concepts of conventional economics. The views of modern science completely dominate it. In spite of the admirable progress of the natural sciences, which spiritual science absolutely does not deny, conventional science rejects everything that arises out of the spirit. Economists want to observe only economic activity. Observation of the economy is almost impossible in modern times because recent human development has rendered people increasingly incapable of having thoughts consistent with economic facts. Economic events proceed almost mechanically; people do not follow them with their thoughts. As a result, observations of these thoughtless events of the world market do not result in economic principles, because our economy is practical action without theory, viewpoint, concept, or idea. On the other hand, the Social Democratic movement is theory without practical application. Taken as it is, socialist theory can never be practically applied because it is a theory with no insight into practicality. In modern times we suffer because on the one hand we have economic life, a practice without ideas, and on the other we have only social democratic theories with no possibility of practice. In this connection, we have truly arrived at a turning point in human historical development. Since the necessary foundation of society is the relationships between people, you will easily understand that a particular attitude must underlie people's goals when they want to create a socially just life. You can also see that the goal of the threefold social organism is to create a certain attitude toward the relationships existing within society. Without such an attitude between people, society cannot truly flourish. Social threefolding definitely takes this attitude into account. Today, I would like to mention only a few anecdotal things in this regard.

If you think of social life as an organism, then you must imagine that, in a spiritual sense, something flows through this organism. Just as blood carries the inhaled and transformed air through the human or animal organism, there must also be something that circulates and flows throughout society.

We now come to an area that is so difficult for modern people to understand because they are so little prepared for it in their feelings. However, we need to understand it if we are to speak seriously about social renewal or the reconstruction of society. We need to understand that social life in the future depends upon cooperative support between people, something done when we exchange our ideas, perceptions, and feelings. Human viewpoints are of no little importance if people want to be social beings. The future requires that we base general education upon concepts that can serve as a foundation for Imaginative thoughts, not just upon ideas taken from science or industry. As improbable as this may seem now, in the future we will be unable to properly interact socially if we do not teach people Imaginative concepts. That is, if we do not teach concepts that affect human feeling much differently than the abstract natural scientific concepts of cause and effect, force and material, and so forth. In the future, we will be unable to begin anything social with those scientific concepts that influence everything today, even art. In the future, we must learn to understand the world in pictures.

I have often given an example of that in connection with education. I said that when we are actively involved with children, we can, for example, teach them the idea of the immortality of the soul simply by showing them a cocoon. You can let them see how it opens, how the butterfly flies out. We then explain to the children that the cocoon is like our body, and that there is something like the butterfly living within it, only it is invisible. When we die, then the "butterfly" flies out into the spiritual world. We act pictorially through such analogies. However, we must do more than simply invent such analogies. If you merely invent such analogies, you would be acting with a conventional scientific attitude. What is the attitude of conventionally educated people when they create such an analogy? People today are terribly clever even before they are mature. They give no thought to the possibility of being wise in a way other than they imagine themselves to be with their abstract concepts. Today, people certainly have strange ideas about "wisdom"!

A few weeks ago, a political science society held a meeting immediately after one of my lectures.[5] At that meeting, a university professor spoke about my lecture and ideas connected with it. He is, of course, a wise man of the present. In his opinion the views presented in the lecture and in all of my books were infantile, only childish. I can well understand how a wise man of the present could come to such a conclusion, particularly if he is a professor at the university. I can understand that because we have squeezed all truly pictorial life out of academic life, so that academics perceive everything understood, or perhaps I should say, not understood, as childish. This is just what is so extraordinary about modern wisdom. If we want to use a picture like the one I just presented about immortality with the butterfly flying out of the cocoon, they say, "We are wise and, of course, we know that it is only a picture. We are above such pictures. However, children are only children, and we need to create such pictures of our concepts for them, though we do not believe in them." What they do not comprehend is that the children do not believe them either, because children become really engrossed in the picture only when you believe it yourself.

Spiritual science brings us back to an attitude that not only let's us see those fantastic things spoken of by natural science, but also let's us again see the pictorial, the Imaginative. The picture of the butterfly emerging from the cocoon is, in truth, a picture of the immortality of the soul, placed into nature by divine forces. There would not be a butterfly emerging from a cocoon if there were no immortal soul. A picture cannot exist—and that is a picture—if truth does not form the basis for it. It is the same throughout nature. What natural science provides is simply fantasy. We can understand nature only when we know it is a picture of something else.

People will need to accustom themselves to seeing, for example, the human head as a picture of a heavenly body. The human head is not round just so it can resemble a cabbage. The head has its shape because it is fashioned after a heavenly body. All of nature is pictorial, and we need to find our way into this imagery. If we do, then what flows into us when we grasp pictures will radiate into our hearts, souls, feelings—even into our heads, although this is the most difficult. In the social organism, we will need to speak to one another pictorially. People will need to believe in these pictures. Then economists will emerge who can speak with truth about commodity within the social organism. Commodities reflect human needs. We cannot comprehend the social value of human needs through abstract concepts. We can comprehend it only through human feeling permeated by an attitude arising from Imaginative thinking. Otherwise, we will not achieve a human society. In the social organism, you could employ people to determine needs, but if you do not at the same time educate people to think Imaginatively, you will never achieve an organic social structure. We must speak pictorially. As strange as it may sound to modern socialists, to create a humane society, people must speak in pictures that excite the Imagination.

That is what is important. People will understand commodity in a feeling manner only through an economics that understands pictures.

In society, the society of the future, a proper understanding of labor must predominate. The way modern people speak about labor is ridiculous because labor has essentially nothing to do with the production of commodities. Karl Marx called commodities "crystallized labor." That is simply ridiculous. What we refer to as "human labor" is the particular way people use themselves up, consume themselves. You can consume yourself in one of several ways. You can, for example, if you have enough money in the bank or in your pocket, participate in sports and use your labor in sports. You could also chop wood or do something else. You could use exactly the same amount of labor chopping wood or participating in sports. Social life depends not upon the amount of labor you do, but upon the use of that labor. Labor has nothing to do with social life insofar as commodities are produced. In the threefold social organism it will, therefore, be necessary to have a reason to work other than the production of commodities. We must, to a certain extent, produce commodities through work because we must use work for something. However, the basic reason people work must lie in their desire to work and their love of work. We cannot achieve a humane society until we can bring it about that people work because they want to work and realize that work is necessary.

That can occur only in a society where people speak of Inspired concepts. In contrast to the past when things were more instinctive and atavistic, in the future people will not glow with a desire and love for work if society is not permeated with ideas and feelings brought to the world through the Inspiration of initiates. People must carry these concepts to become aware that they have before them a social organism to which they must dedicate themselves. That means that a desire to work will exist in people's souls because they understand the social organism. People will gain such understanding only when they are spoken to through Inspired concepts, that is, through spiritual science. For a desire to work to arise, we need concepts from spiritual science that can permeate people's hearts and souls, not those empty concepts often spoken of today. Spiritual science will permeate people's hearts and souls so that they have a desire and love for work. Labor will take its proper place alongside commodity within a society that hears not only of pictures from teachers, but also of Inspirations and those concepts necessary in our complicated society to provide the means of production. That will give people the proper foundation upon which to build.

Intuitive concepts must also spread in that society. You can find those concepts in my book *Towards Social Renewal*, in the chapter about capital. They can blossom only in a society receptive to them. That means that capital can take its proper place in the social organism only when people admit they need Intuition. Commodities will take their proper place when people admit they need Imagination, and labor will take its proper place when people admit they need Inspiration.

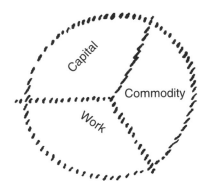

If you do not write these three concepts under one another, but write them in the way I have done in this diagram, and comprehend all three of those concepts, you can learn a great deal. There are interrelationships between labor and commodity, and between commodity and capital to the extent that capital purchases commodities. Relationships exist between labor and capital and so forth, but you must connect those three concepts as I did in the diagram.

We need to understand the truth of stating that a human attitude must permeate society in the future. People themselves must create society as they become accustomed to hearing about Imagination, Inspiration, and Intuition from the science of initiation. That is a serious point. I am saying nothing less to you than that a future reformation of society cannot occur without spiritual science, and that is the truth. People will never be able to understand the necessity of Intuition, Imagination, and Inspiration if you leave the schools to the state. What does the state do with schools?

Think of something primarily connected to schools and the state, for example, public law.[6] I must admit I find it terrible, but modern people do not notice it. Public law should arise out of those things people perceive in their souls as correct. Here, I only want to look at democracies and will not address the case of a monarchy. Public law arises through parliaments, which pass laws for the state. Every adult citizen is connected with public law through his or her representative. Things are decided and enter the body of public law. Then, along comes a professor who has studied public law and teaches the laws passed by the parliaments as, of course, public law. Thus, the state pulls academia along behind it in this area. A professor of public law does not teach anything other than what exists as law in the state. We would not even need a professor if we were able to reproduce the laws on phonograph records. We could simply place a phonograph at the podium and allow it to play back the laws passed by the parliament. That is what academia has become.

That is only an extreme case. You can see it is certainly nothing Inspired because you could hardly claim that what modern parliaments decide constitute Inspired deeds. Things need to be reversed. At the universities, public law should be taught from a basis of human spiritual understanding. Only then can people give the state its proper form. Many people believe the idea of the threefold social organism would stand the world on its head. Perish the thought! The world is already standing on its head, and the threefold social organism would only put it back on its feet. That is what is important.

It is important to find your way to an understanding of such concepts; otherwise, we will go in the direction of a mechanization of the spirit, an anesthetizing or vegetation of the soul, and an animalization or instinctive form of the body.

It is important to be convinced that we need to think in such a radical way if the future is to blossom healthily. We need to recognize the necessity of a social organism based upon three healthy realms. People will learn how Imagination is connected to commodities only if economic life is clearly defined, and we recognize the need to administer economic life with fraternity. What Inspiration means for labor—that it calls forth a desire and love for work—will exist in the world only when Inspiration permeates the concept of equality in parliaments so that equality truly prevails and individuals can validate what lies within themselves. However, that will be quite different for each person. Then, equality will prevail in the rights realm. Laws will be Inspired and not passed in the mundane fashion increasingly common to democracy.

We can properly value capital in the social organism only when Intuition rises to freedom and freedom blooms from the developing spiritual life. Then, what work needs will flow to it from spiritual life.

Streams will flow as my arrows indicate in the diagram, and the three areas of life will be so integrated that they properly permeate each other.

Cultural Life
Freedom
Intuition

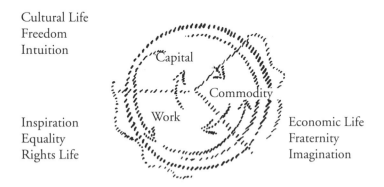

Capital

Commodity

Work

Inspiration
Equality
Rights Life

Economic Life
Fraternity
Imagination

In this connection, one of the first objections I encountered in Germany was that people said I wanted to divide social life into three parts, while social life needs to be unified. This kind of unification hypnotizes people because they have always viewed the state as all-encompassing. They are accustomed to the concepts of a bureaucratic state. Someone who says something about such unity seems to me to be like someone who says that I want some old nag to stand on four feet, but we must keep the old nag unified and cannot divide her into four legs. Of course, no one would expect that, but I am also not interested in putting the old nag "state" or the social organism upon only one leg. It must stand upon three healthy legs. Just as a horse does not lose its wholeness when it stands upon four legs, the social organism does not become disconnected when placed upon three sound legs. The social organism becomes a unity precisely because it is founded upon three sound realms. Modern people simply cannot break with their habitual concepts. Now it is important that we do not believe we need simply to change external appearances, but that we recognize we must reform our ideas, concepts, and feelings. In a way, we could say we need new heads to work toward a truly healthy future for humanity. We really do need different heads on our shoulders. People have such difficulty getting used to new ideas because they love their old heads so much, those old heads so accustomed to thinking the way people have thought for so long. We need to consciously reform what now lives in our souls. Do not expect that to be an easy task. Many people believe they have already changed their concepts and do not notice that the old remain, particularly in the area of education. Strange things happen. You can talk to people about the pedagogical concepts arising from spiritual science. You talk with very progressive teachers, school directors, and so forth. Then, after they have listened, they say they have thought the same for a long time, they are of exactly the same opinion. In truth, though, their opinion is exactly the opposite of what you have said. They have exactly the opposite opinion, but they use the same words to express that contradictory opinion. Imagine it, they use the same words and say something with exactly the opposite meaning! That is how modern people pass one another by. Words have long lost their connection with spirituality, but we absolutely must find this connection again. Otherwise, we will not move forward.

Social tasks lie much more in the realm of the soul than we usually think.

LECTURE FOUR

DORNACH / AUGUST 15, 1919

FROM WHAT I SAID previously, you will certainly have recognized that the question of education is the most important question occupying people today. I needed to emphasize that education is central to our social problems. After my lecture a week ago concerning reforming and transforming the school system, you will certainly understand that the most important question in education is that of teacher training. If you consider the character of the period that clearly began in the middle of the fifteenth century, you will certainly have an impression of human development undergoing waves of materialistic ordeals. Now, our greatest need is to work ourselves out of that materialism and find a path back to a more spiritual attitude. In all previous periods of human culture, people knew the path toward spirituality, but they knew it more or less instinctively and unconsciously. Humanity lost that knowledge so that we could seek it again in a completely conscious manner, motivated by our desire to find our own freedom.

The transition humanity has undergone since the middle of the fifteenth century could be called the materialistic ordeal of humanity. If you consider the character of that materialistic time and then consider with some insight the cultural development of the last three or four centuries into our own time, you will find that the materialistic wave that broke in upon humanity has affected the education of teachers most intensely. Nothing could make as lasting an impression as the way materialism has permeated pedagogy. We need only look rationally at some specific examples of modern teaching methods to see the great difficulties lying in the way of achieving truly fruitful progress. We need but recall how those who believe themselves particularly capable of speaking about education continually repeat that all education, beginning at the lowest level, must be illustrative, or at least what people call illustrative. I have often mentioned that people want, for instance, to make arithmetic illustrative by using mechanical devices. People place such great value upon allowing children first to "see" everything, and then, from this visualization, to create a picture or idea in their own souls. The desire for visualization is certainly justifiable in many areas of education, but it forces us to question what will happen to children after they have been educated through this "visual" teaching method. If we teach children only according to that "visual," "hands-on" method, they will become completely withered in their souls. The power within their souls will slowly die, and human nature will become connected with that visualized environment. The tender shoot which should grow within the soul will slowly die. Much of the modern illustrative teaching method results in the death of the soul. Of course, people do not know they are killing the soul; nevertheless, it dies. We can already experience the result in people today. Just look at how many modern adults have what we might call troubled natures. Look at how many cannot find anything within themselves that could give them consolation and hope in difficult times and enable them to cope with the complexities of life. Today, we see many broken people, and we even see, at least at times, that we ourselves cannot find our way in life.

This all relates to the deficiencies in our education, in particular, to the deficiencies in the training of teachers. What do we need to do to improve teacher training? That teachers know the answers to questions put to them in their examinations is relatively unimportant, since they are mostly answers the teacher could look up as needed in nearly any reference book. However, what the examinations completely ignore is the general condition of the teacher's soul, something that continuously transfers to the pupils. There is an enormous difference between what happens when one teacher enters the classroom and what happens when another enters. When one teacher steps into the classroom, the children feel a kind of inner soul relationship with the teacher. When another teacher enters, the children often feel no such relationship. To the contrary, they often feel a gulf between themselves and their teacher, and experience all possible shades of indifference to the point of laughing at or deriding the teacher. All the nuances lying between those two extremes often exist, to the detriment of genuine teaching and education.

The burning question is, therefore, how can we change teacher training in the future? No change is possible unless the teacher accepts the knowledge of human nature that comes from spiritual science. The relationship of human beings to the supersensible worlds must completely permeate the teacher. He or she must be able to see in the growing child proof that the child has entered earthly life from the supersensible world through birth, has clothed itself with a physical body. The teacher must be able to see that the child has taken on tasks that the teacher is to assist with here in the physical world because the child could not take on those tasks during the period before rebirth.

The teacher must feel that he or she should perceive each child as a question posed by the supersensible world to the

sense-perceptible world. You cannot ask that question in a concrete and comprehensive manner, that is, in relation to each
individual child, unless you can use the knowledge of spiritual
science about the nature of the human being. In the course of
the last three or four centuries, people have become more and
more accustomed to looking only at human physiology and at
the human physical constitution. That is the most detrimental
viewpoint for the teacher. For that reason, it is of utmost necessity that in the future, pedagogy take root in the anthropology
arising out of Anthroposophy. That is, however, not possible
unless we understand the human being as a being consisting of
three aspects, as we have often mentioned here from many perspectives. However, you must commit yourself to a true inner
comprehension of these three aspects. I have repeatedly pointed
out the various ways human beings, as they stand before us
now, can be seen as nerve-sense beings. We commonly express
this by saying that someone is "all head." We find, at least
superficially, the second aspect of human nature, namely, the
chest being, in those people in whom rhythmic processes predominate. Then, as you know, we have that aspect of the
human being connected with the metabolism, namely, the limb
or metabolic human being in which the metabolism as such
occurs. The complete external picture, the complete physical
form of the active human being is of a being composed of these
three aspects.

To summarize, the three aspects of human nature are: the
head or nerve being, the chest or rhythmic being, and the limb
or, in its broadest sense, of course, the metabolic being.

The question is, how should we understand the differences
between these three aspects of human nature? That is something that makes modern people uncomfortable, since they like
to divide things mechanically. If you say to someone that the
human being consists of a head, a chest, and a limb being, they

want to draw a line at the neck and call what lies above, the head being. They then want to draw another line somewhere else to delineate the chest being, and, thus, have the different aspects placed one after the other. Modern people do not easily accept things they cannot mechanically describe.

However, in reality things are not so simple, since there are no such lines. It is true that the human being above the shoulders is primarily a head or sense-nerve being; however, it is so not only above the shoulders. For example, the senses of touch or temperature spread out over the entire body. In the same way, the head aspect extends out over the entire body. If you want to speak that way, you could say that the human head is primarily head and that the chest is less so; nevertheless, the chest also presents aspects of the head. The limbs, or everything that has to do with the metabolism, are even less so; nevertheless, the head aspect also appears in them. Thus, we would have to say that the entire human being is head, but the head is primarily head. If we wanted to draw that schematically, then we would need to draw the head aspect of the human being in this manner [shown as white in the sketch].

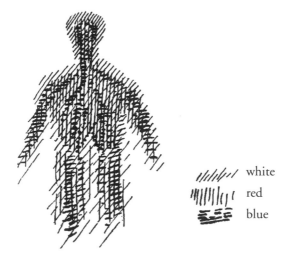

white
red
blue

The chest aspect of the human being is again not only in the chest, although it is primarily in the organs contained within the chest, in those organs that most clearly express the heart and breathing rhythms. However, breathing continues into the head and the blood circulation continues its rhythm into the head and limbs. We can, therefore, say that the human being is, of course, chest in this region [shown as red in the sketch], but also here in the head, although less, and here in the limbs still less. Thus, the entire human being is chest, but this [pointing to the chest in the sketch] is primarily the chest and that, the head.

Again, the limb or metabolic aspect of the human being is primarily here [shown as blue in the sketch], but the limbs continue and are somewhat less in the chest region and least in the head.

Just as we can say that the head is head, we can state just as truthfully that the entire human being is head. Just as we can say that the chest is chest, we can state just as truthfully that the entire human being is chest, and so forth. In reality, these things intermingle. However, our understanding tends to want to put things next to one another and to separate the various aspects. That shows us how little our cognitive ideas relate to external reality. In external reality, things flow into one another, and we must be aware that when we separate the head, chest, and metabolic aspects of the human being, we also have to think of these separated aspects as a whole. We may never think of things only in their constituent parts, but must also think of them united. A person who would want to think of things only in their parts is the same as someone who would want only to inhale and never to exhale.

There you have something similar to what must occur for the future in the thinking of teachers. Teachers must be particularly adept at this kind of inwardly mobile thinking, this non-mechanical kind of thinking. Only when they accustom themselves to this kind of fluid thinking can they approach reality with their souls. However, people cannot approach reality if they cannot grasp things from a larger perspective than is currently fashionable. When viewing things scientifically, people will need to overcome the prevailing modern habit of looking only at the details and learn to connect the details with the larger questions of life.

The question of immortality will become an important question for all further development of spiritual culture in the future. We will need to become clear about how a large portion of humanity understands immortality, particularly now when many people have gone so far as to deny immortality. What is it that lives in many people today who attempt to understand immortality from the basis of the more common religions? What lives in those people is a need to know something about what happens to the soul when a human being passes through the gate of death.

If we ask why people are interested in the question of immortality, or perhaps better said, the question of the eternal life at the core of human nature, we receive no answer other than that they mainly want to know what happens when people pass through the gate of death. People know that they have an I and that in this I lives their thinking, feeling and willing. The thought that this I might be destroyed is, for them, unbearable. What people want to know is that we can carry the I through death and what happens to the I after death. The interest people have in that question arises from the fact that religions, at least the ones under consideration here, mainly speak of immortality or eternal human life in answer to the question of what happens to the human soul when a person passes through the gate of death.

Now, you certainly must feel that the question of immortality, when posed that way, leaves an extremely strong egotistical aftertaste. It is a fundamentally selfish desire that arises within people when they want to know what happens to the essence of their being as they pass through the gate of death. If modern people had greater self-awareness, they would consider the question more carefully, and not give in to such illusions. People would see how strongly egotism acts in their interest to learn about the fate of the soul after death.

That kind of attitude within the soul became particularly strong during the period of materialistic trials that occurred in the last three or four centuries. We cannot overcome what has grasped the human soul in its habits of feeling and thinking through, for instance, theories or hypotheses, so long as these theories and hypotheses are abstract. Nevertheless, we most certainly must ask, "Can things remain like this?" That is, can the selfish aspect of human nature have the only say about the question of the eternal existence of the essence of a human being?

If you look at everything connected with that complex of questions, then you must admit that the reason the human soul has the attitude I just described is essentially that religions have failed to take up another perspective. They have failed to look at how the soul increasingly permeates the physical body when a human being is born, how it grows into the world at the baby's first cry. They have failed to look at what lives within human beings in the spiritual world before birth. How often today do we hear the question about what continues from the spiritual realms when a human being is born and enters physical existence? What we hear time and again is the question of what is carried forward when the human being dies. We rarely hear the question of what is carried forward when a human being is born.

In the future, we will need to give more attention to that question. In a certain sense, we must learn to hear the revelation of the spirit-soul of growing children, and how it was before birth. We must learn to see in growing children the continuation of their stay in the spiritual world. Then, our relationship to eternal human nature will become less and less egotistical. If you have no interest in what continues from the spiritual world in physical life but are only interested in what continues after death, then you are inwardly egotistical. In a certain sense, the foundation of a selfless attitude within the soul exists in looking at how we carry the spiritual world into physical existence.

Due to their egotism, people do not ask about that continuation, because they are certain they exist and are content with that idea. People are only uncertain that they will exist after death, and therefore want to have it proven. It is their selfishness that leads to that. However, true understanding will not occur through human egotism, not even from that subtle egotism we have just characterized as creating interest in the continued existence of the soul after death. Can we deny that religions reckon with that form of egotism? We must overcome that kind of selfish speculation. Those who can look into the spiritual world know that overcoming that speculation will bring not just greater understanding, it will bring an entirely different attitude of people toward their surroundings. People will feel and perceive children much differently when they see in them a continuation of something that could no longer remain in the spiritual world.

Think for a moment how the question changes when viewed from that standpoint. We could then say that a human being existed in the spiritual world before he or she moved through birth into the physical world. There, it must have been that the individual could no longer reach his or her goal. The spiritual world could no longer provide what the individual's soul needed. As the time for birth approached, a need thus arose to move from the spiritual world into the physical and to take on a physical body to seek in the physical world what the individual could no longer find in the spiritual.

You will acquire a tremendous depth of understanding of life if you know how to use this standpoint, to use it with feeling and perception. Whereas the egotistical standpoint causes people to become increasingly abstract, to pursue the theoretical and tend toward head-bound thinking, what arises from the other perspective, the selfless perspective, causes people to recognize and comprehend the world through increasing love. That is one of the elements we must bring into the education of teachers, namely, to look at prenatal human existence and not consider only the riddle of death. Teachers also need to have a feeling for life in connection with the riddle of birth.

We must also learn to raise anthropology to the level of Anthroposophy by acquiring a feeling for the forms that express the three aspects of the human being. Recently, I posed the question whether the human head, that is, that part of the human being that is primarily head and is spherical, is merely set upon the remainder of the organism. If we then look at the human chest aspect, how does it appear to us? The human chest is such that we could take a portion of the head, and if we were to enlarge it, then we would have the backbone. The head has its center within itself, but the center of the human chest lies very far away. If you think of that "head" to which the chest belongs as extremely large, you will see that this large head resembles that of a person lying on his or her back. If we think of the spinal column as an incomplete head, we would have a horizontally lying person and a vertically standing person.

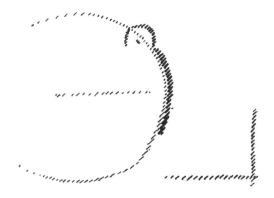

When we look at the metabolic aspect of the human being, it becomes so complicated that we can no longer draw it on a plane. In short, concerning their forms, the three aspects of human nature present themselves quite differently. The head is complete, whereas the chest aspect is incomplete and only a fragment. And then, we have the metabolic aspect!

Now, why is the human head complete? It is complete because of all the human aspects, the human head is the best adjusted to the physical world. Regardless of how unusual that may sound to you, since you customarily consider the human head the most noble aspect of the human being, it is nevertheless correct that it is best adapted to physical existence. It best expresses physical existence. Thus, if we want to find the primary characteristics of the human body, we must first look toward the head since the human head is the most physical part of the body. The human chest and rhythmic organs are most closely connected with the etheric body, and the metabolic organs most connected with the astral body. The I has no clear expression in the physical world at all.

We have now come to something that is particularly important to look at closely and that you should thoroughly understand. You should understand that when you look at the human head, that is, what I drew in white, you have before you the most important aspect of the physical human body. The head most completely expresses the visible human being. The etheric body is more active in the human chest aspect. The etheric body is least active in the head and most active in the chest. Therefore, from a physical perspective, the human chest aspect is less complete than the head, physically less complete. The metabolic aspect of the human being is certainly very incomplete because there the etheric body is active only very little and the astral body is most active. As I have often emphasized, the I is still a baby and has barely any physical correspondence.

Thus, you see that we can describe a human being by saying that human beings have a physical body. If you question what portion of the human being is most like the physical body, the answer is, the spherical head. The human being also exists in the etheric body. What most closely resembles the etheric body? The chest fragment. The human being also has an astral body. And what most closely resembles the astral body? The metabolic human aspect. It is hardly possible to point to something corresponding to the I in the physical human being. Thus, each of the three aspects of the human being, namely, head or sense-nerve being, the chest or rhythmical being, and the metabolic being, becomes a picture for something standing behind it. The head is a picture of the physical body, the chest, of the etheric body, and the metabolic system, of the astral body. That is what people must learn—not to consider people in the manner done so often today, whereby a corpse is examined and some piece of flesh is considered in one way or another independent of whether it exists in the chest or in the head. People will need to learn that the head, chest, and metabolic aspects of human beings relate differently to the cosmos and provide a pictorial expression of the different things that they represent. In that way, we will extend today's simply anthropological manner of observation into Anthroposophy.

The chest and head organs are equivalent when considered purely physically. Whether you examine the lung or the brain is unimportant from a material perspective; however, from a spiritual perspective, that is not at all the case. From a spiritual perspective, if you dissect the brain, you really have fairly clearly before you what you dissect. If you dissect the chest, for example the lungs, what you have before you is much less clear, since the etheric body plays such a tremendously important role there during the time people sleep.

What I have just discussed has a spiritual counterpart. Those who have made progress through the meditations and exercises you can find described in our literature slowly come to understand that the human being truly exists in three aspects. As you know, I have spoken of these three aspects from a certain standpoint in the chapter of my book *How to Know Higher Worlds* where I speak of the Guardians of the Threshold. However, you can also achieve a picture of the three aspects through strong concentration upon yourself. You can actually separate the head, chest, and metabolic aspects. You will then see why your head is the head you have. If, through inner concentration, you separate your head with all its component parts from the remainder of the organism, so that it is uninfluenced by the other aspects of human nature, it is dead and lives no more. It is impossible to separate clairvoyantly the head from the remainder of the human organism without perceiving it as a corpse. You can do that with the chest aspect, and it remains alive. If you separate the astral body by separating the metabolic aspect of the human being, then it will run from you. It remains in place no longer, but follows cosmic movements, because the astral body has that tendency.

Now, imagine standing before a human child and observing him or her objectively and soberly as I just discussed. You look at the head, and it contains death within it. You look at what

affects the head from the chest and see that it enlivens everything. You look at the child beginning to run, and you recognize
that it is actually the astral body that is active in that running.
Now, the human essence becomes somewhat more transparent
for you inwardly. The head, a corpse. The outspreading of life in
the human being, quiet when the person is still. At the moment
the child begins to run, you immediately notice that it is actually
the astral body that runs. The child can run because the astral
body is running, and in moving, it consumes material. Thus, the
metabolism is active in a certain sense. But the I, how can we
observe that? We have truly run out of possibilities. After we
have considered the head-corpse, the life-spending chest aspect,
and running, what remains so that we could externally look at
the I? As I said, the I hardly has a physical counterpart. You can
only see the I when you look at human beings in their continuing growth. At the age of one, they are quite small, at two, larger,
and so forth. When you see them growing larger and larger and
add to it everything that occurs during the ensuing stages, you
see the I physically. You never see the human I when you just
look at a person, you can see it only when you see the person
growing. If people would not give in to illusions, but instead
would see reality, then it would be clear that they could not easily perceive the I physically. You can see the I only when you
look at a person at different ages in life. If you see someone after
twenty years, then you perceive that person's I quite strongly in
the changes that occurred, particularly if you saw that person
twenty years before as a child.

You should not consider what I have just said simply theo-
retically, but use it to enliven your thinking. When you look
at a person-head as corpse, chest as enlivening, movement as
the astral body, growth as the I—consider how that enlivens
the entire person who previously stood before you like a porcelain doll.

What of the human being do people usually see with their physical eyes and comprehend with their intellect? Simply a porcelain doll! That comes alive when you add to it what I have just discussed!

Of course, you need to permeate your view with what spiritual science can provide for your feelings and perceptions concerning the relationship of the human being to the world. A running child reveals its astral body to you, for what lies in the gesture of running, and every child runs differently, comes from the individual's astral body. What lies in growth is imprinted by the I.

Here you can see how karma strongly affects the human being. Let us take an example no longer closely connected with the present, namely, Johann Gottlieb Fichte. I have described him from various perspectives.[1] At other times, I have described him as a great philosopher, as a Bolshevist, and so forth. However, let us look at him from still another standpoint. You will recall how I showed that we could certainly consider Fichte a Bolshevist, but we now want to look at him in a different way. Suppose we were to stand out in the street, and Fichte went by. We would look at him and think to ourselves that he is not a very large man, rather stocky. What does the way he grew reveal to us? Suppressed growth. When we look at the way he walks, we see how he stamps along on his heels. There we see the entire Fichte-I. You would not miss the slightest detail of what the man was as you watch him stamp along on his heels and see his suppressed growth, his stocky, compact body caused by malnutrition in his youth. You could hear how he spoke by observing him from behind!

A spiritual element can come into the externalities of life. However, that is not possible if people do not have a different attitude than currently exists in their souls. Looking at their neighbors that way would be a very unkind indiscretion for modern people. Modern people do not like to be looked at that way because they are mainly formed by materialism and its way of spreading. They do not open letters not addressed to them only because it is prohibited, otherwise they would open them. People with that attitude find it unacceptable that everything might be different. Nevertheless, since the middle of the fifteenth century, the Earth has achieved what people cannot reach in earthly existence unless they comprehend the human being spiritually, right into the physical. As we move into the future, we will need to learn how to spiritually comprehend everything sense-perceptible. That must begin with the pedagogical activity of the teachers in relationship to the growing child. Physiognomically oriented pedagogy requires that teachers have the will to solve the greatest human riddle of each individual through education!

Perhaps now you can feel how strong are what I called "the trials of humanity" in our times. What I discussed increasingly compels us to consider each person an individual human being. That must hover above us as a great ideal, namely, no one is like anyone else and everyone is an individual being. Were the Earth to achieve its goal without us recognizing the individuality of each human being, then humanity would not reach its goal upon Earth. However, today we are certainly far from the attitude that strives toward that goal! Today, we make everyone the same and see people such that we do not consider their individual characteristics. I have often spoken of Hermann Bahr.[2] Once in Berlin, he told how people no longer see others as individuals. During the 1890s he lived in Berlin for a time and was active in Berlin society. He, of course, had a woman seated to the left and one to the right at dinner every evening. However, as he sat between two different women on succeeding evenings, he noticed that he could tell they were different women only because of the place cards. He did not look at them very closely because the woman from yesterday and the one from today were essentially the same. What he saw was just the same. Our industrial society makes people externally all the same and does not allow an expression of individuality. In this way, modern people move toward stereotypes, whereas the innermost human goal must be to strive toward recognition of the individual. At present, we attempt to camouflage individuality, but it is essential that we seek it.

Directing the inner view of the soul toward a recognition of the individual must begin with education. The education of teachers must assume the attitude of seeking the individuality in each person. That is only possible if we enliven our idea of the human being as I have presented it today. We must become truly conscious that it is not simply a mechanism that moves us, it is the astral body, which carries the physical body along with it. Compare what arises in your soul inwardly enlivened, a moving picture of the entire human being, with what conventional science now provides, pure illusion! Science says nothing about the human being, but simply preaches illusions. We must bring the true human being into pedagogy, but now it is totally left out.

The problem of education is actually a problem of training teachers. As long as we do not see that, we are not so far along that something fruitful can occur in education. Seen from a higher perspective, everything is connected. Today, people prefer to develop human capacities, the inner capacities of human beings, as separate subjects. People learn anthropology and then religion, but they do not learn the relationship of one to the other. In reality, as you have seen, the consideration of the human being is related to the question of immortality and eternal human nature. We must bring that question into direct connection with our view of human beings. In particular, we must bring the flexibility of experience within the soul. We will then develop inner capacities quite different from those developed today in the teachers' colleges. That is of particular importance.

In my considerations today, I wanted to show you that spiritual science must permeate everything. We cannot solve the great social problems of the present without spiritual science.

LECTURE FIVE

DORNACH / AUGUST 16, 1919

IN OUR DISCUSSIONS we need to include an ever widening consideration of history, of how cosmic forces are imbedded in the stream of modern development and how they form the basis of human life. From our discussions yesterday, you will have seen that, if humanity is to progress, we increasingly need to transform our customary fixed and abstract modern concepts into fluid, mobile, living concepts. A consideration of the facts concerning those human soul forces we call intelligence can shed particular light upon that. As you know, modern people are particularly proud of their intelligence. They deem intelligence to be, in a sense, something that in the course of time has made significant progress.

When we look back upon earlier times, and see that people then often imagined things pictorially, that they attempted to comprehend through myths, legends, and so forth things that we now believe we understand through intellect, we might think that those earlier people had childish spirits or souls. Today, we look back upon the childlike stages of human development and remark about how much we have achieved, particularly in the development of intelligence. In a way, today's discussion is devoted to the peculiarities of human intelligence, and concentrates on those soul forces of which modern people are particularly proud. When people now speak of intelligence, they hold a specific picture of a force within the soul. They think intelligence can and should be only the way they habitually think of it.

In earlier stages of development, people had intelligence, though of a different sort. To understand the meaning of what modern people call intelligence, we must ask how people in earlier developmental stages viewed intelligence, and how that intelligence slowly changed into the form we find in our times.

Today, we do not want to go back any further than the time we normally call the Third post-Atlantean period, the Egypto-Chaldean period, which was followed by the Greco-Roman period, and then by our age. In particular, we want to consider the characteristics of intelligence in the ancient Egyptians, the Chaldeans, Greeks, and Romans, and then go on to consider the particular kind of intelligence that exists among us in the Fifth post-Atlantean period. As you can see, I am assuming that it is incorrect, and it *is* incorrect, when people think intelligence is simply intelligence and is only possible in one form, that is, that someone who has our form of intelligence is intelligent and someone who does not, is not. That is simply not true. Intelligence goes through metamorphoses and transformation. It was different during the Egypto-Chaldean time from the way it is now. We can best visualize intelligence at that time when we recognize that the ancient Egyptians and Chaldeans instinctively comprehended the relationship of their human essence to the entire cosmos through their form of intelligence.

The things that modern people reflect upon through their intelligence were not even thought about by the Egypto-Chaldean people, because they did not have the same kind of intelligence. When they thought, when they brought their intelligence into motion, their connection with the cosmos lived in that intelligence. The ancient Egyptians and Chaldeans knew how they stood in relationship to one or another of the zodiacal signs, they recognized the influence of the moon and the sun and the other planets upon their souls and their bodily constitution. They knew how the rhythms of the seasons affected their nature. They comprehended all that through their intelligence, and they gained a complete inner picture of their relationship to the cosmos through their intelligence.

Intelligence changed as the Egypto-Chaldean period of humanity came to a close in the eighth century before Christ. Slowly, intelligence became something quite different from that of Egypto-Chaldean times. Intelligence began to lose the complete comprehension of its connection with the cosmos. That understanding ceased to exist as completely as it had before the eighth century B.C. People were still aware of a connection to the cosmos, but they knew it more as a kind of echo, or a kind of memory of what earlier people knew. In its place, a thinking arose in Greek intelligence that was more about human beings themselves, so that people had less relationship to the cosmos and were more inhabitants of the Earth. The Greeks had a clear feeling and a clear perception of that through their intelligence. Through that intelligence, they comprehended all that occurred in mortal earthly life.

That feeling was then lost through the development of intelligence that began in the middle of the fifteenth century, that is, with the beginning of the Fifth post-Atlantean period. If the Greeks wanted to understand something supersensible, they knew they had to turn to looking, to a kind of looking that existed more or less atavistically in the pre-Christian era and still existed in the Greeks. They knew that through reflection and through intelligence, they could only learn about the principles and laws that form the foundation of everything that exists and dies in mortal life. "If I am to understand the living,

I must look." So said Plato's students. That is, "If I only think, I can only comprehend what is dead."

The Greek occult schools examined a particular subject in this regard. They examined approximately the following situation: "Everything is spiritual, even those things that appear material have spiritual processes and spiritual principles at their foundation. Those things that appear to be of an earthly material character are also fundamentally ruled by spiritual law. There are spiritual laws to which you are subject because you are physical. To the extent that you live in physical existence and then pass through the gates of death, your body will give itself over to material forces and to the material of the Earth. However, these material forces and earthly matter only seem material. They are also spiritual, but permeated by those spirits that appear to you as death. If, through your intelligence, you comprehend any laws, those are the laws of death. They are the laws of those forces that are contained within graves and that receive corpses." Many Greek occult students became convinced that human intelligence can comprehend only those things that are received by graves and that hold corpses. The occult teachers told their students that if they wanted to know about the spiritual realm they live in while on Earth, or about the realm they live in with a disembodied soul between death and rebirth, then they must receive what they see with conviction. If they were not convinced of what they saw, but instead developed concepts and ideas through their intelligence, they would comprehend only the material spirit that receives their physical bodies.

In his or her intelligence the Egypto-Chaldean human being perceived and felt a relationship with the entire cosmos, but the Greek intelligence perceived what ruled the grave. Our intelligence also perceives only what rules the grave, but we do not know that. Those of us who study such things go into dissection rooms and probe corpses, thus learning the principles of corpses that our intelligence can comprehend. Then we make them into the principles of human beings. Those are, however, only principles of the grave. Our intelligence comprehends only principles of the grave.

About the time of the transition during the middle of the fifteenth century, intelligence changed again. We are now only at the beginning of this change and transformation of intelligence. Our intelligence goes along a particular path. Today, the development of intelligence that began with the Greeks still strongly envelops us. Through our intelligence, we comprehend only the underlying death. However, that kind of death-comprehending intelligence is changing. In the next centuries and millennia, intelligence will become something different, something vastly different. Our modern intelligence already has a certain tendency. As human beings, our intelligence will further develop so that it will tend to comprehend only what is false, to comprehend only errors and illusions and to think only about evil things.

Occult students and, in particular, initiates have known for some time that human intelligence is developing toward evil, and that it will become more and more difficult to recognize good simply through intelligence. Humanity is now undergoing that change. It is now barely possible for people, when they exert their intelligence and are not carried away by especially wild instincts, to still look toward the light of what is good. However, human intelligence will more and more tend to conceive evil and to integrate that evil into human morality and knowledge, creating error.

That is one of the reasons why the initiates called themselves people of anxiety, because in fact, if you consider the one-sidedness of human development that I just mentioned, you will become anxious. You will become anxious because of the development of intelligence. It is certainly not for no reason at all that so much pride and aloofness has entered into the intelligence of modern people. That is a kind of prelude to the way intelligence is becoming evil in our Fifth post-Atlantean period, which is now only beginning. If people develop nothing more than their intelligence, they will become evil beings upon the Earth. When we look to the future of humanity and want to think of that future as healthy, we may not rely upon that one-sided development of intelligence. During the Egypto-Chaldean period, intelligence was something good, but then it became connected with the forces of death. In the future, intelligence will enter a relationship with the forces of error, illusion, and evil.

This is something about which humanity should have no illusions. Humanity needs to recognize objectively that we must protect ourselves against a one-sided development of intelligence. There is, of course, a reason why something else has arisen through anthroposophically oriented spiritual science, namely an acceptance of what we can achieve through a renewal in looking at the spiritual world, something we cannot comprehend through intelligence. We can comprehend it only when people embrace what the science of initiation can bring from the spiritual world through seeing.

However, we also need objectivity for that, and here we confront a deep mystery, particularly in Christian esoteric development. Had the Mystery of Golgotha not occurred in earthly development, it would be unavoidable that people would fall to become evil beings living in error due to their intelligence. The Mystery of Golgotha is not simply a teaching or a theory or a view of the world or a religion that arose during the development of humanity. Something did, in fact, occur through the Mystery of Golgotha. That superearthly Being, Christ, lived in the human being, Jesus of Nazareth. Since Christ lived in Jesus of Nazareth, and Jesus died, the Christ Being then entered earthly development. The Earth now contains the Christ Being. We need only be conscious of that as an objective fact, a fact that has nothing to do with what we subjectively understand or feel. We must know it for the sake of our knowledge. We must accept it into our ethical culture for the sake of our morality. Christ has entered into human development and, since the Resurrection, lives there, primarily in our soul forces. Grasp the full depth of this fact!

Look at the difference between people who lived before and those who lived after the Mystery of Golgotha. Certainly, they are the same people, because souls go through repeated earthly lives. However, when we look at human beings as earthly beings, we have to differentiate between those humans who lived before and those who lived after the Mystery of Golgotha.

You see, if you look for a general understanding of God, that understanding is not the same as a comprehension of Christ. You can achieve a general understanding of God by going out and looking at things in nature. If you look at the physical human being to the extent you can observe it externally, you can achieve it. However, you can only approach the Christ Being if you discover something within yourself during earthly life. You can find a general understanding of God by simply saying to yourself that you have come into earthly existence from cosmic forces. However, you can find an understanding of Christ only if you go further than nature allows. If, during your existence in the world, you do not find an understanding of God, this lack of understanding is a kind of illness. A healthy person is never really an atheist. An atheist would in one way or another be ill, either in body or soul. That illness often reveals itself only through the fact that a person is an atheist.

However, not knowing Christ is not an illness, it is a misfortune, a missed opportunity. If you reflect upon the fact that you were born out of nature and out of nature's forces, then, with a healthy soul, you can then achieve an understanding of God. If you experience something like a rebirth during your life, then you can achieve an understanding of Christ. Birth leads us to God, rebirth to Christ. Before the Mystery of Golgotha, human beings could not find within themselves that rebirth through which people can find Christ. That is the difference toward which I ask you to direct your attention, namely, that human beings before the Mystery of Golgotha could not find that rebirth and could not understand that Christ lived within them, because Christ had not yet entered humanity. Since the Mystery of Golgotha, that is now possible. Human beings can find the spark of Christ within themselves if they exert themselves during life.

In that rebirth, in finding the spark of Christ in ourselves in an upright and honest ability to say, "Not I, but Christ in me," lies the possibility of not allowing the intellect to fall into deception and evil. That is the higher meaning of salvation in an esoteric Christian sense. We need to develop our intelligence since we cannot become less intelligent. However, we stand before the temptation to fall into error and evil when we attempt to develop our intelligence. We can escape that temptation only by gaining a feeling for what the Mystery of Golgotha brought into human development.

It is absolutely true that people have a possibility of escaping evil and error only in Christ Consciousness and in being united with Christ. Egypto-Chaldean people did not need a rebirth in Christ because they still felt a relationship to the cosmos through their natural intelligence. The Greeks had the seriousness of death before them when they used their intelligence. Now, however, people live at the beginning of an age when intelligence will become evil if they do not permeate their souls with Christ as Strength. When you think about that, you will see that it is a very serious matter. It shows us how we should understand certain things that begin to appear in our time, how we should think about the fact that people in our time will develop a tendency toward evil because they are moving toward a further development of their intelligence. It would, of course, be completely false to believe we should suppress our intelligence. We should not suppress intelligence, but in the future, those with insight will need a certain kind of courage to use it, because that intelligence brings with it the temptation toward evil and error. We will need to find a way to transform intelligence by permeating it with Christ as Principle. Human intelligence will become entirely Ahrimanic if Christ does not permeate human souls as Principle.

You can see how much of what I have just described is now beginning to be visible in modern human development and is visible to people with insight. Recall what the third aspect of human development, threatening humanity through materialism, brings to people today. If you remember how much cruelty exists within modern cultural development, a cruelty barely comparable to that of barbarian times, you will hardly doubt that the demise of intelligence has clearly begun. We should not look at modern cultural developments superficially, nor should we doubt that modern people who want to work toward healthier development should attempt to achieve a true comprehension of the Christ Impulse. Today, there are two things we can clearly see. One is that very intelligent people tend toward evil, and the other is that many people unconsciously suppress that tendency by allowing their intelligence to sleep, thereby not fighting against it. At the present, there is clearly a sleepiness in human souls or, in those souls that are awake, a strong tendency toward evil and error.

You may recall that I mentioned in a previous lecture that children born in the last five, six, seven years are different from children born earlier. Those who look closely can see a clearly melancholic shadow in their faces. I said that arises because modern souls do not want to come into an earthly existence so filled with materialism. You could even say that before birth souls have a kind of anxiousness about entering the world, a world where intelligence so tends toward evil and where people are so caught up in a downward developmental spiral.

Teachers need to develop a consciousness of that. Children are different today than they were some decades ago. This is clear even from superficial observation. Children need us to teach them differently than they were taught some decades ago. Teachers need to educate children with an awareness that what they are really doing is saving the children, and that they need to bring the children a way of finding Christ as an Impulse in the course of their lives, that is, of finding their own rebirth.

Such things cannot develop in teaching when, for example, you have only a simple, theoretical comprehension of them; they develop in teaching only when your soul is strongly affected by them. We must particularly expect teachers' souls to be strongly affected by an awareness of the temptation that intellect brings to humanity. The pride modern people have developed for their intellect could take a grave toll upon humanity were it not held in check through what I have just discussed. That is, if we do not balance our pride in the intellect with a strong and energetic awareness that the best thing for us as human beings in this and following incarnations is that we find what of Christ exists in us as Impulse.

Now, you must, of course, be aware that you will not find Christ as Impulse in the dogmatism of some religious group. Since the middle of the fifteenth century, the churches have done more to distance humanity from the Christ Impulse than to bring humanity to it. Religions make all kinds of promises, but in doing that, they do not bring Christ to people as

Impulse. Since the Mystery of Golgotha, people need to feel that everything their inner selves can reveal to them is connected with the meaning of the Mystery of Golgotha for the Earth. If you perceive the meaning for the Earth of the Mystery of Golgotha, you can recognize that the development of the Earth would be senseless if human beings now fall into evil and error through their intelligence. If you perceive the meaning of the Mystery of Golgotha in that way, you will also see how senseless earthly development would be without the Mystery of Golgotha.

If you decide to do something today or in the future to teach and educate human beings, you need to be very strongly permeated with that thought. People need to accept this general perspective, but you certainly know how far modern people are from accepting it. Thus, nothing is more necessary than to point out again and again not only the importance of spiritual scientific principles, but also the seriousness that must fill our souls so that we may learn the corresponding facts in human development through spiritual science. Not only our knowledge, but our entire life should receive the impulse of spiritual science. If you do not feel that seriousness, you will not be a spiritual scientist.

I would ask that you give particular attention to what a spiritual scientific foundation reveals, namely, that human intelligence, left to itself, will drift toward the Ahrimanic path and that we can direct it toward the good only by accepting Christ as the true Impulse. I believe that those who accept the full seriousness of this truth will also bring that seriousness into the relationships they develop to the various modern points of view and philosophical streams. Here there is very much to do.

People who come from various areas of Eastern Europe often relate with particular disgust a fact that certainly does not point to positive developments along the path of civilization. What I refer to is the presence of the so-called "Gun-Toting Women." This is a specific group of women now emerging in Eastern Europe, Eastern European women used in the revolutionary movements there. People who do not belong to the ruling party there are often imprisoned or killed and thus always fear for their lives. In some parts of the East, young women, armed with old guns left over from the war, are responsible for shooting those people opposed to the government now in control. These "Gun-Toting Women" dress up in stolen clothing, they "dress to kill," and enjoy carrying their rifles and shooting people. They like to brag about it, about how it feels to see blood spurting from young people, and how older people's blood looks. These are the kinds of ghastly situations we find in modern civilization. The existence of "Gun Women" is one of the proud achievements of the present!

We need to point out such things. They are there to cause us to look at the underside of the seriousness of our times. Certainly, we do not need to know about every aberration of our so-called progressive culture to feel the earnestness with which we should apply ourselves to present-day problems. That seriousness should arise in us simply through an understanding of human development itself. We would hope that the sleep in which humanity now finds itself will change into an awakening. That awakening can result only from a comprehension of the seriousness of the task presented to people today. These aberrations indicate the dangers presented by an intellect left to itself and steering toward an Ahrimanic path. That should be the impulse that arouses a feeling in us for the seriousness of the problem.

LECTURE SIX

DORNACH / AUGUST 17, 1919

YESTERDAY, I discussed the path human intellect and intelligence will need to take in the future. I based that discussion upon specific facts brought to light through spiritual scientific activity, a few of which I want to mention today. In a practical sense, you need to be aware that when a human being stands before you, that human being is the being of whom we speak in Anthroposophy. As you know from my book *Theosophy*, that means we must always be aware that we have a being of four aspects before us. We have the I, the astral body, etheric body, and physical body. Although we have these four aspects of human nature present each time a person stands before us, from the common point of view, modern people actually do not know what is before them. People simply do not know. They think what stands before them is the physical body. However, we cannot see what is physical in the physical body in the same way we normally see things with our eyes. What we see with our eyes as the physical body and the way it stands before us, we see only because the etheric and astral bodies and the I permeate it. As strange as it may sound, the physical body is only a corpse during our life between birth and death. Only when we have a human corpse before us do we, in truth, have the physical human body. When you see a corpse, you see the physical human being without the etheric and astral bodies and the I. They have left the physical body and we can, therefore, see it in its true nature. You will have an incorrect picture if you believe the physical human being is something you carry around with you in physical space. Your picture will be much more correct if you think of a corpse and realize that your I, your astral body and your etheric body carry that corpse around.

An awareness of the true nature of the human being will become more and more important in our time. Things were not always as they are, and have been for quite some time, in the present stage of human development. Of course, we cannot derive the things I tell you through ordinary physical science; however, spiritual scientific understanding shows them to be so. If you go back to the eighth century before Christ, which, as you know, is the beginning of the Fourth post-Atlantean period, you would be in the Egypto-Chaldean period. At that time, the human body had different characteristics than it does today. The human bodies now displayed in museums as mummies were, in subtle ways, quite different from human bodies of today. They carried within them a greater plant-like quality and were not nearly the complete corpse of the modern human body. In their physical constitution, human beings were much more similar to a plant, whereas since the Greco-Roman Period the modern human physical body is more similar to the mineral kingdom. If, through some cosmic wonder, we were to receive the same bodies as those of the Egypto-Chaldean population, we would all be ill because we would have rampantly growing tissue within our bodies. Many illnesses are caused by the fact that the human body sometimes atavistically returns to the state that was normal in the Egypto-Chaldean period. Today, tumorous growths occur in some people because a portion of their body tends to become like the entire body of the Egypto-Chaldean.

This has an important connection to human development. As human beings, we now carry a corpse around with us. However, the Egyptians did not do that. They carried something similar to a plant around with them. The result was that their understanding of things was different from ours, and their intelligence functioned differently than does ours. I would ask you to consider carefully the question of what it is that people understand through modern science, a science of which they are so terribly proud? It is only death! Science repeatedly emphasizes that normal intelligence cannot comprehend life. Some researchers believe they will someday completely understand the complicated combinations of atoms and molecules and their interactions with life by performing more and more chemical experiments. That will never happen. Through chemistry and physics, we will understand only what is mineral and dead, that is, we will comprehend the living only to the extent it is a corpse.

In spite of everything, human cognitive intelligence is a part of the physical body, that is, a part of a corpse. What does that corpse we carry around with us actually do? It brings us the furthest in mathematical and geometrical understanding. Everything is transparent there, but things become ever less transparent the further we go from mathematics and geometry. That is because today the human corpse is the cognitive aspect in us, and what is dead can comprehend only what is dead. The etheric and astral bodies and the I do not play a role in modern human cognition; they remain in the dark. If the etheric body could perceive in the same way that the physical body perceives what is dead, it would perceive what lives in the plant world. That is what was so remarkable in the plant-like bodies of the Egyptians, namely, that the Egyptians could perceive the plant world much differently than modern people do. We can trace much of our instinctive understanding about the plant world back to Egyptian insight arising from their instinctive consciousness and embodied within their culture. We still base much of our modern botanical medical knowledge upon the traditions of ancient Egyptian wisdom. You know that a number of so-called lodges not founded upon genuine fundamentals call themselves Egyptian lodges. That is because they look back to Egypt when they want to impart specific knowledge. However, that knowledge is no longer very valuable. In such circles, traditions based upon wisdom obtained through the Egyptian body still live. As people slowly moved into the Greco-Roman age, the living human plant-body slowly died. The human plantlike aspect died during the Hellenic Age or, at least, was gradually dying then. We carry a dead body within us and that death is particularly appropriate for the human head. I have mentioned from numerous points of view that initiates perceive the human head as a corpse, as something dead, as something in a continuous process of dying. Humanity will become more and more conscious that we perceive only through a corpse and, therefore, we perceive only things that are dead.

As we move into the future, an increasingly intense desire will arise to again perceive the living. However, people will not be able to perceive the living through normal intelligence, bound as it is to a corpse. Many things must happen for people to regain the ability to penetrate the world in a living way. Today we need to understand everything human beings have lost. When human beings moved from the Atlantean period into the post-Atlantean period, they could not do much that modern people can do. For instance, since a certain time in your childhood, each one of you can say "I" to refer to yourself. You say this "I" quite without a feeling of respect. In the course of human development, "I" was not always said with such lack of respect. In earlier periods of human development, and this was still partially true in ancient Egypt, although it had to an extent subsided, there was a name that expressed what we now express with the word "I," but when that name was spoken, it stunned people. For that reason, they avoided saying that name. If the population living just after the Atlantean catastrophe had experienced the speaking of that name for the I, a name known only to initiates, all those who heard it would have been stunned. They would have collapsed because that name for the I would have had such a strong affect upon them.

That fact still resonated into ancient Hebraic time when only initiates were to speak the Unspeakable Name of God or to present it to the population in a kind of eurythmy. The Unspeakable Name of God originated in what I just told you, but humanity gradually lost that feeling and the deep effects arising from it subsided. During the First post-Atlantean period, the I had a deep effect. In the Second post-Atlantean period, the astral body had a deep effect. In the Third post-Atlantean period, the etheric body had a deep, but at least bearable, effect, one that brought people into a relationship with all creation, as I mentioned yesterday. Now, we can say "I" and all sorts of things, but they no longer have an effect upon us because we comprehend the world through our corpse, that is, we comprehend the dead, the mineral part of the world. However, we must regain the desire to return to those regions where we can comprehend the living. During the Greco-Roman period, from the eighth century before Christ until the middle of the fifteenth century, all human development moved toward ever greater dead understanding of the corpse. Now intelligence moves along the path I spoke of yesterday. That is why we must resist naked intelligence and must add something to it.

In a way, we need to properly retrace our path. During the Fifth post-Atlantean period we need to learn to perceive the plant aspect, in the Sixth, the animal aspect and only in the Seventh, the true human aspect of life. Thus, the task of modern humanity is to move beyond simply understanding the mineral to understanding the plant.

After you have understood that, consider who most exemplifies a person seeking that plant knowledge: Goethe. To the extent that his activity was contrary to that of conventional science and its preoccupation with things dead, and instead moved toward the living, toward metamorphosis and the development of plants, he was a man of the primitive beginnings of the Fifth post-Atlantean period. If you read Goethe's essay of 1790, "The Metamorphosis of Plants,"[1] you will find that Goethe gradually attempted to comprehend the plant, not as something dead or complete, but as something developing from leaf to leaf. You will see there the beginning of the kind of understanding we should seek, particularly in this Fifth post-Atlantean period.

Thus, Goetheanism sets the basic tone for what we should seek during this Fifth post-Atlantean period. In a way, conventional science must awaken in the Goethean sense, and must move from concern with things dead to those living. That is what I mean when I continually repeat that we need to move away from dead, abstract concepts and into living, concrete concepts. What I said yesterday and the day before was basically a description of the path along which we can move into living, concrete concepts.

We cannot move into such concepts and ideas if we do not unite our views of the world and of life. Today, under our particular cultural circumstances, we have to allow the differing streams of our world view to course, disconnected, alongside one another. Consider for a moment how a person's religious world view often runs, disconnected, alongside his or her scientific world view. Many people have the one and the other but build no bridges between them. They often have a kind of fear or anxiety about creating these bridges, but we must be quite conscious that things can remain so no longer.

During my present visit with you, I have discussed how egotistically people now form their world views. I said that modern people's interest lies primarily in the life of the soul after death, and it is purely out of their egotism that their primary interest lies in that direction. I described how we must slowly redirect interest toward the life of the soul beginning at birth, to the extent this is a continuation of life before birth. Were we to consider the development of the child in the physical world as a continuation of prenatal spirit and soul existence with the same interest and desire to understand now reserved for life after death, our understanding of the world would take on a much less egotistical character than it has today. However, the selfish character of our present world view is related to many other things. At this point, modern people need to gain greater clarity about the true basis of that fact. Until now, human beings have primarily developed selfishness. The I has permeated both the world perspective and the will. We should have no illusions in that regard. That has occurred most conspicuously in the religious confessions. You can easily see that religious confessions have become egotistical. Consider, for example, how modern preachers are taught to deal with human egotism. The more preachers take people's selfishness into account and make promises about the life of the soul after death, the better they achieve their goal. Today, people do not really have much interest in anything else. They certainly have little interest in that living spiritual activity that previously existed in the spiritual world and is now so wonderfully visible in the soul after birth.

The way members of the various religious confessions think about God is the result. That they place God in the highest position does not, in fact, say very much. What is important is that we remove all illusions in that connection. What do most modern people mean when they say "God"? What kind of being do they refer to when they speak of God? What they mean is an Angel, their own Angel, which they call God! Nothing more! People still have a vague feeling that they have their own guardian spirit, which they look up to and call God. Even when they do not call it an Angel, but God, they still only mean an Angel. That people do not get beyond an Angel with their concept of God is due to the egotism of the religious confessions. The reason for that is the narrowing of interests caused by egotism. We see the limitations of interests clearly in modern public life.

What do people often ask about today? Do they often seek to understand the fate of humanity? Today, it is very sad to speak to people about the fate of humanity. They have no idea that these things have changed so much in a relatively short time. You can, for instance, tell people that mighty spiritual battles, the like of which humanity has never before seen, will follow the war of the past four or five years. Those battles will occur because those things the West calls maya or ideology, the East calls reality, and what the East calls reality, the West calls ideology. Today, you can draw people's attention to such important facts, but they have no awareness that saying the same thing a hundred years ago would have affected people's souls such that they could not have freed themselves of it!

That change in humanity, people's indifference regarding the fate of humanity, is one of the most visible phenomena. Nothing affects people today. They accept the most comprehensive, decisive, intense statements with indifference and are hardly bothered. That is because people's interests are increasingly limited by a stronger and stronger intellectual egotism. Thus, even though we now have such good democracies and parliaments, when these parliaments assemble, questions concerning the fate of humanity do not arise because the people elected to parliament have little concern for the fate of humanity. Only selfish interests arise. Everyone has his or her own selfish interest.

People form groups based upon the similarities of their superficial professional interests. When such groups become large enough, they form majorities. Thus, questions of human fate do not arise in parliaments or other representative forms, only egotistical questions multiplied by so and so many people. Even religious confession has moved into the realm of egotism because only egotism lives in modern human beings. Religious confession will experience the necessary re-enlivening only when human interests become broader, that is, when people can again look beyond their own personal fates to that of humanity.

Religion will be enlivened only when people are again strongly concerned when someone tells them that a different culture blooms in the West than in the East and in the middle still another than at the poles of East and West. People must understand what it means that people in the West seek the great goals of humanity, when they seek them at all, by turning toward mediums who enter a kind of trance, thus inducing a semiconscious subearthly connection with the spiritual world.[2] Western people then allow such mediums to inform them about great historical goals. You can say that as often as you want in Europe, but Europeans do not believe that there are societies in the Anglo-American countries that attempt to find mediums, to get them into a trance, and then to obtain answers about the great fate of humanity through cleverly posed questions. Western people will also not believe that in the East, people do not seek answers to questions concerning the fate of humanity through mediums, but through mystics. Today, that is so real you can almost touch it.

Everywhere you can find the beautiful speeches of Rabindranath Tagore in which you can read how people from the East think about the general goals of humanity. Westerners read those speeches the same way they read a column by some hack writer because they cannot tell the difference between a newspaper hack and someone of such great spirituality as Rabindranath Tagore[3]. People are unaware that different cultural groups live next to one another. I have spoken for years in my public lectures about what is important for Middle Europe,[4] but none of it was understood as was necessary.

The intent of what I just said was to indicate the possibility of becoming aware of things beyond your own fate, of things connected with the fate of groups of human beings, so that you can concretely differentiate between them. If you raise the sight of your soul to an understanding and comprehension of humanity throughout the Earth and attain an intense interest for things beyond your own personal fate, you create within your soul a capacity to comprehend something higher, something more real than an Angel, namely, an Archangel. You will not have thoughts about the nature of an Archangel if you remain only in regions of concern to egotistical human beings. If preachers give sermons only out of the realm of selfish human beings, they can speak as much as they want about God and Divinity, but they actually speak only about Angels. That people call them something else is simply an untruth and does not change the situation from what it, in fact, is. Only when you begin to acquire an interest in human fate connected with space can your soul come into that attitude that lifts it to understand an Archangel.

Let us now go on to something else. Feel within yourselves the impulses arising from the various stages of human development. Feel within yourselves the fact that a large number of our present leaders were educated in classical schools during the time the human soul can receive a certain kind of flexibility. They were educated in those schools that arose not out of our modern culture but instead out of a previous culture, that of the Greeks and Romans. If the Greeks and Romans had done as we do now, they would have created schools based upon the Egypto-Chaldean culture. They did not do that. Instead, they took their subject matter directly from life. We, however, take it from a previous period and educate people accordingly. This has significant consequences for human beings, but we have not recognized them. Had we recognized its significance, then the women's movement would have a different tone than now exists. The women's movement would sound a note that would convey something like the following. We send men to antiquated schools to develop a particular capacity of intelligence, and, thus, their brains become hardened and embittered. As women, we have had the good fortune of not being allowed into such schools. We want to give our intelligence its original timbre. We want to show what we can develop for the present when we do not deaden our brains in youth with a Greco-Roman education.

That tone does not exist. On the contrary, the more common tone is that we have subjected men to Greco-Roman education, and now we women want that, too. We, too, will receive a classical education.

People have so little understanding for what is genuinely necessary. We need to understand that in our modern time we are not educating people for the present, but for the Greek and Roman period. That is why that culture is still so prevalent in our lives. You can feel it. You can feel the Greco-Roman culture living in our leaders of the present time, you can feel it living in what people call intelligence and in intellectuals. That is one attitude living among us today, something we carry in the entirety of our mental development. We cannot read a newspaper without being affected by Greco-Roman education because we write in a Greco-Roman style, even when we write in our own local dialect.

Concerning our ideas of law and justice, as I have mentioned before, we actually live within Roman culture, something also antiquated. The culture of Rome is alive in our laws. Occasionally, the old common law still struggles against that of Rome, but without success. People should feel that what officials now refer to as just and unjust is simply the glimmer of the now far distant past.

Only in economics do we live in the present. That says a great deal and, therefore, there is much we need to change. If I may make an aside here, many women use modern concepts—but they use them only in cooking, that is, in managing the household. To that extent, they are actually people of the present. Everything else we bring into the present is outdated. I am not saying that the conceptual aspect of cooking is a particularly desirable goal, but it is definitely not very desirable that modern women also leave the present and return to the cultures of antiquity. Therefore, when we look at what exists within our culture, we have to look not only at those things active in space, but also at those acting out of the distant past. If you develop a feeling for that, you will see how not only the past but also the future affects us. It is, in fact, our task to allow the future to affect us. Although only a weak awareness of it exists, we would certainly be in a very sorry state if every person did not rebel against Greek culture and Roman justice, and if the future could not shine in upon us.

To understand our culture, we must take time as well as space into account. We must consider not only what history brings to us from the past, but also the future. We should be aware that, to the extent that we are people of the present day, both the past and future play a role in our souls. As Europeans, we need to be aware that not only America, England, Asia, China, and India, not only the two poles of East and West, affect us, but Greece, Rome, and the future as well. As we become accustomed to considering how the latter affects us, how the past and future live in our souls, a different soul attitude will arise that goes beyond an egotistical consideration of human fate. An attitude that goes beyond simple spatial considerations will arise. When we have developed that attitude in our souls, we will be capable of developing concepts about the Time Spirits, the Archai. Then we will come to the third level of the divine hierarchy. It would be good if, through the means I just described, people would allow themselves to perceive these three hierarchies in concepts and ideas. The Spirits of Form that then follow are endlessly more difficult to grasp.

It is sufficient for modern people to attempt to penetrate beyond egotism into the realm of the non-egotistical, to try time and again to penetrate what I have just described. That is particularly important for educating teachers. We should not allow teachers to teach before they have gained a concept of the selfishness that strives toward the nearest god, that is, toward the Angel. We should not allow teachers to teach before they have achieved an idea of those non-egotistical forces that determine human fate and exist spatially distributed over the Earth, that is, of the nature of the Archangels. Nor should we allow them to teach before they have gained an idea of how the past and the future affect our culture, how Roman law and the Greek spirit affect us, and how that undefined rebel of the future can save us.

Today, people have little desire to look at such things. Some time ago I often said that among the social tasks before us is that of taking the content of the education children receive in the upper grades from the present. That is, it is our social task to do just what, in end effect, the Greeks themselves did, namely, to take the subject matter from the present.

In the same town where I spoke about this and other important social problems, there appeared soon afterward—I do not want to imply a direct connection, although this is certainly of symptomatic significance—there appeared in all that town's newspapers announcements about the local classical school. Here I had held some lectures describing my thoughts on high school education, and then announcements appeared in the newspaper about how proud we should be of the youth attending that school, about how the education they received "strengthened national consciousness," and developed "national strength" and so forth. All this only a few weeks before the Treaty of Versailles! These announcements were signed by all manner of locally renowned people, from the schools and the department of education. Unfortunately, what we say from a true basis of human development simply bounces off. People always allow it simply to bounce off them, and it does not touch them in the depths of their souls.

That is one of the difficulties in social activity. People will never master our modern social tasks with the prevailing superficial attempts. Questions about the foundation and development of society have deep importance and cannot be answered if people are unwilling to look into the depths of humanity and into the nature of the world. For the very reason that the situation is as it is, you can see the necessity of the changes arising from a threefolding of the social organism.

People must develop an organ to sense the needs of our times. It will be difficult to develop such an organ in the spiritual or cultural realm because, as I have already said, the state has gradually swallowed up cultural development in education. The state has filtered the desire for activity and active striving out of human beings and has made then into dutiful members of the state organization. I think I also posed the question here about how the great majority of people live. There are, of course, exceptions, but until approximately the age of six, people live unhindered because they are still too dirty for the state. The state is not eager to take on *that* necessary task with young children; it leaves that task to others. However, afterward, children are taken over by the state and are trained to become proper members of the state and to fit into the molds foreseen for them. Children stop being human and become simply what the state says they are. They then become something for the state.

People want that because they are constantly told the state will give them room and board not only while they work, but even beyond, that they will receive a pension until they die. That is the ideal for many people today, namely, to have a position that will later result in a pension. The religions continue in the same direction, promising a pension even after death, that is, the soul receives a right to a pension. People are told that without any activity on their part, their souls will receive immortality simply through the activity of the church. The church will take care of that! Of course, it makes people uncomfortable to hear that they must seek salvation in free spiritual activity, activity that must be independent of the state, and that the state should concern itself only with the rights between people. It makes them uncomfortable to hear that the state will not provide a pension. That causes many people to reject this idea. You can see that again and again.

For the most intimate portion of spiritual life, namely, religious life, a world view directed toward the future will require that people earn their immortality, that they allow their souls to be active so that they can receive God and Christ through that activity.

I've received many, many letters during my life, often from members of various churches who say that although Anthroposophy is very nice, it contradicts the simple, Christian belief that Christ saved human souls and that through Him we can receive eternal salvation with no activity on the part of our souls. They cannot let go of the "simple belief in salvation through Christ." People believe that when they say or write such things, they are particularly pious. However, they are simply egotistical. They are selfish right down to the very foundations of their souls. They desire to do nothing in their souls and to let Divinity take care of them so that their souls receive a wonderful pension on the other side of the pearly gates.

It is not so easy in that world view that requires us to create a new idea of religion. People must realize that they have to work to understand the Divine in their souls. They cannot just passively subjugate themselves to churches that promise to take care of their souls. Something that once caused distress but that is no longer practiced, namely, caring for the soul in return for money, still plays a hidden role. What we need, but do not particularly love, is to move toward inner activity and toward a life connected with all creation, of which we count ourselves a part.

To acquire a feeling for what we need in this area, we must see some of the things I mentioned today in our souls. We must recognize the metamorphosis of human beings since the time of the ancient Egyptians. We must understand that at that time the body had more of a plant-like nature, so that when our bodies today fall back into that state, they become ill and cause the growth of cancerous tumors. We must understand that we carry a corpse around with us. Through such things, we can gain a feeling for what humanity needs, namely, to truly move forward regarding the questions of society. We can no longer allow ourselves to view the problems of society in the most simplistic manner.

That is one of the most difficult things today. You must be aware that one of the greatest modern difficulties is people's desire to have some of the most important questions about life explained to them in a few abstract sentences. If something like my book *Towards Social Renewal* contains more than a few abstract sentences, if it contains the results of observing life, then people say they do not understand it. It even seems confused to them. However, the misfortune of the present day is that people have no desire to examine those things in need of examination. Abstract sentences that are quite transparent concern only death. However, what is social is living. We must have flexible points of view, we must use flexible sentences, we must create flexible forms. That is why, as I have often said, we should not consider simply a change in particular conditions, but, instead, we must get used to rethinking and relearning the innermost connections of our thinking and reflecting.

Now that I will be leaving for a few weeks, that is the thought I wish to leave with you. That is where we need to feel ourselves in our common anthroposophical and social activity. I want more and more understanding to arise about how Anthroposophy is to enter into human souls if we are to achieve anything in the social realm. I hope you can carry in your hearts something I have often said in various ways. We need to recognize the knowledge we can gain through Anthroposophy as the true measure of our activities and desires of the present, and we need the courage to instill Anthroposophy into them. The worst thing is that modern people have so little courage to really comprehend what is necessary. They allow the best forces of their wills to collapse. They have no desire to act, necessary though that is.

You should learn to represent Anthroposophy with courage so that people will look upon our building[5] here, the representative of our spiritual desires, with interest. Take joy in each individual who shows even a little understanding. Meet that person. Do not take it to heart if you are met by people of ill will or, what occurs more often, by people lacking understanding. What is important is to have the courage to continue. We

should consider ourselves a small group destined by fate to know
certain things and to give those things so needed in today's
world. People may laugh at us and say that is presumptuous. It
is, nevertheless, true. To say to yourselves, "It is, nevertheless,
true," in all seriousness, so that truth fills your soul, requires the
inner courage we must have. May that permeate us as the sub-
stance of Anthroposophy. Then, we will do what we need to do,
each of us in our own place. That is what I want to tell you
today. The fact is that, in a sense, we want to wish ourselves past
each day that brings us closer to the activity we will achieve for
the world through our building here. This building is the only
building that in its form takes the destiny of humanity into
account. We can rejoice in the fact that there is some attention
given to it; however, more is needed for fruitful progress regarding the questions of society. Something like our building, with
its stark forms, so different from other modern architectural
forms, can spiritually improve the powers of humanity. We want
human beings to become open once more for what we want
them to know so that they can rise, not only to the Angels, but
to the Archangels and to the Spirit of Our Time.

I must now take leave of you for a few weeks. I hope we will
then be able to continue this discussion, and that you will continue your energetic activity for our building. You see, my dear
friends, it is evident from all sides in the outer world that what
human beings need is a desire and willingness to work. They
will not have that if they are not convinced of the great goals
before them. I believe that when people become convinced
they can achieve an existence more worthy of a human being
through the threefolding of the social organism, they will again
begin to work. Otherwise, they will only continue to strike.
People today need such a desire, need such a motive that grips
them in the depths of their souls. That is true in the area of
physical work.

We will not be able to give modern humanity a motive to spiritually overcome what is simply dead if we do not show that our work on at least *one* object can be fruitful and shine out into the world. Please consider that until we meet here and can speak together again. Auf Wiedersehen!

[With these words Rudolf Steiner left Dornach to travel to Stuttgart where, two days later, he began the cycle of lectures and seminars that serve as the foundation for Waldorf school pedagogy.]

PART II

BACKGROUNDS OF
WALDORF EDUCATION

PROLETARIAN DEMANDS

AND HOW TO PUT THEM INTO PRACTICE

A Lecture to the Employees of the Waldorf-Astoria Factory

STUTTGART, APRIL 23, 1919

WE LIVE IN A VERY SIGNIFICANT TIME. This is reflected in the events resounding throughout Europe, events that will become more widely significant. This important moment requires widespread serious contemplation about the tasks confronting working people, about essential human rights, and about what life in general should offer. So that we can consider these things seriously, I need to say some introductory words.

During your lives, most of you have formed some opinion about how to solve the so-called social question, an opinion about what the social movement should do. Workers will need to rethink much of that opinion. We confront very different things now than we did just a short time ago, and so we must think very differently now and in the near future. Today, I want to speak about how we must begin to think. First, however, we must agree that it is most important for us to trust one another, because out of trust we can truly create something. Trust has dwindled recently—at a time when many possibilities manifested in the terrible catastrophe they caused. In Europe, that catastrophe, conservatively estimated, resulted in ten to twelve million human deaths and three times as many disabled. We can see in those results how wrongly humanity's current leaders thought and acted. Today, from a completely different class of people—the proletariat—a thoroughly justifiable demand arises. This is why the proletariat is confronted with very different tasks today than it was even a short while ago.

In order to indicate some of these tasks, I want to mention what certain Social Democratic leaders said shortly before the October and November catastrophes in Germany.[1] They said that once the war is over the German government would have to deal with the proletariat much differently than before—that in all of its dealings and in all of its laws the government would have to consider the proletariat. The government would no longer be able to treat the proletariat as they had previously. That is what the leading Social Democrats said only a relatively short time ago. But, what does that mean? It means that shortly before the November revolution the Social Democratic leaders assumed that the old German government would rule again following the war.

Now, however, we are faced with the fact that the government has been swept away, both here in Central Europe and in much of the rest of Europe. It is thus obvious that government cannot take social demands into account. Consequently, we must speak today very differently about these things than even the most insightful, well-intentioned Social Democrats were recently able to do. Today, what confronts the proletarian is the need to create something reasonable out of the present chaos and confusion. For this reason we must now look at things very differently.

Only a short while ago, if someone had spoken to you as I do now, you would have paid attention to what was said. You would have looked to see if what was said was generally consistent with the social ideas or ideals of the proletariat, and you would have rejected them if, in general, they were not. Today, however, we have to do things differently, otherwise we will not only fail to move out of chaos and confusion, but will fall more deeply into it. We must instead use something very different to awaken trust in one another. Today we must look at *intent*. We need to find out whether someone's words are intended in an honest and upright manner. Today, we must allow everyone to speak about what we should do—regardless of their perspective—so long as their intent is honest and upright concerning the demands of the proletariat.

Nowadays, the way we can meet those demands is really a question of secondary importance. The primary question is whether those now speaking about reformation or reconstruction have honest intentions toward the proletariat's demands. We must look at those who speak to see if their intentions are honest—to see whether they are convinced that the proletariat's current demands are justified. Only when people recognize the justification of such demands can they take a position and say how we can fulfill those demands.

You will notice that the "Call to Action," with which most of you are familiar, deviates significantly from previous socialist demands.[2] Nevertheless, I believe that if there is some understanding of that "Call to Action" and of my book, *Towards Social Renewal* (which will appear in a few days), and if people understand the goals, we can achieve what the proletarian movement has wanted for more than half a century, but in a more appropriate and concerted manner. The conditions of our time themselves in a certain sense have given rise to those desires. Things cannot continue as the leading classes have directed them. In criticizing the behavior of those groups of leaders, however, we must find ideas for what we can and must do. The proletariat has prepared itself exceptionally well by forming the new organization demanded in the "Call to Action." Thus, I believe that if we can correct a number of misunderstandings, the proletariat will have the most significant understanding of what needs to be done according to the serious intent of the "Call for Action."

If, rather than thinking *about* the proletariat, you think *with* the proletariat as I have done, you will find that modern economics has completely harnessed the proletariat. No wonder today's proletariat calls to those who utilize the fruits of economic process to fund their so-called "higher culture." No wonder the proletariat tells the leading classes that they, the proletariat, want to create a completely new social order out of economic process. For centuries (but especially during the nineteenth century) the leading classes have harnessed workers to the economy. They occupied the worker so much in economic life and allowed economics to play such a vital role in the worker's life that workers see nothing but economics. Workers see all of their energy absorbed by the economy, and that their energy has created the profits through which the upper class support their so-called higher culture. Workers have seen that they earn only a poor living while others live well. Now, the workers say we must create a new social order based on economics, one that will somehow bring future well-being. Of course, this perspective is inevitable. It is not important that we form an opinion about society based on what we have experienced and grown accustomed to. It is important, however, that we ask what society needs to become genuinely capable of living.

A living social organism must, as its first task, enable every human being to answer, with dignity and respect, the question: What am I as a human being? That task preceded the events that brought us to this difficult time in human history—events nearly as old as today's social movement. It was present before the publication of the "Call to Action." The "Call to Action" did not arise from some flight of fancy, as do the thoughts of many who now develop social programs. It arose from the extent of my own experience of it. Through that experience, I saw that one of the main reasons we are so far behind in answering the most important social questions is that the leading classes have not always been able to find an idea that would place society on its own feet in a healthy way. That, of course, simply cannot be discovered through bourgeois thinking. You can find such thoughts only when you think neither with a bourgeois nor a proletarian attitude, but with a purely human attitude.

Now, you might ask why those who publish the "Call to Action" don't join a socialist party. I can give you a simple answer. I was the one who initially wrote the "Call to Action," and I have never belonged to, nor could I ever belong to, a bourgeois party or association. If I did join some party, they would have to reform all of their programs.

The "Call to Action" begins with a discussion of culture. We need a completely new formation, maybe even a radically new formation, of culture. One who has not worked for many decades within cultural life in the way necessary for its future health cannot easily assess how to form that culture in a healthy and essential way. Certainly, when such things are discussed, we have to speak in extreme terms, and many would reply that things are not really so bad. As for myself, I have never been in a dependent relationship within cultural life. I have never been dependent on the state or other organizations. Throughout my entire life, I have always worked with culture on its own terms. The intent of the "Call to Action" was to state this condition as a general human goal. Those who worked within cultural life in that way, those who never depended on the state or any conventional, superstitious organizations, have experienced things about culture that allow them to understand modern proletarian life. Such people know how difficult it was for the proletariat to throw off the bonds of a culture that has brought so much misfortune—more misfortune than you yourselves, with your socialist attitudes, might believe—especially the ills and suffering of the proletarian body and soul.

In the material realm, in the ordinary realm of economics, people today can be divided into two classes. On the one hand, there is the bourgeois class that now includes the nobility, and on the other hand, there is the proletarian class. Because they have become class-conscious, modern proletarians know what they need. They had no choice about the fact that they are proletarians. They were thrown into the proletarian group by economic processes. Under the old economic and state order, cultural workers could not choose between becoming cultural entrepreneurs or cultural proletarians. Cultural workers could hardly become proletarians if they did not make peace with the ruling classes. In the cultural realm, you could either snake your way through the difficulties that resulted from the old order, or you could make peace with the ruling powers and work culturally as proletarians do in the material realm, but you would not really be proletarian in spirit, but simply a slave. As a cultural worker, you either had to accept everything—all of the rancor of the old order—or, having surrendered to the social structure of the old order, become a slave and worse off than the proletarians.

I do not want to make any personal remarks here, but simply remain objective. However, we have such suffering today because cultural slaves have become mere servants of economics and governmental powers. Since the rise of modern technology and soul-numbing capitalism, modern workers have been harnessed to the economic process. As a result, they cannot view things comprehensively. Those who are not harnessed in that way, but in a more spiritual way, know what is necessary to bring well-being to human development. They recognize that cultural life must be emancipated. They know it is impossible for people to develop the capacities, human talents, and everything human beings bring into the world through birth, while at the same time serving what has resulted in modern times from the government and the economy. The first task is to free culture.

The proletariat has many objections and prejudices about freeing modern culture. The situation is such that modern culture arose along with modern technology and soul-numbing capitalism. A new culture also arose, but in relation to class. This is difficult to understand, so I will give you an example. Twenty years ago I gave a lecture to a group of workers in Berlin. Some middle-class people also attended. There, I stated what for me is self-evident—that not only material things result from the capitalist economic system, but that our science is also a result of capitalism. Most of the proletarian leaders did not believe me at the time. They said that science exists in its own right; what science objectively determines is objectively determined. It doesn't matter whether we consider it from a proletarian or a middle-class perspective. People carry such errors in their heads, regardless of whether they are proletarian or middle class, since the proletariat has adopted the middle-class perspective. Now we are faced with the need to disregard that belief adopted from the middle class. We must instead choose the independent knowledge that develops only when we have overcome our prejudices.

We could say, for example, that we have now happily decided to work toward a unified school. If culture were free, and if there were no longer state-enforced compulsory education, parents could freely decide which school their children would attend. In that case, all the members of the upper classes would establish their own schools. Thus, the old class-oriented schools would exist again. Such an objection might be justified under the old order, but soon it will no longer be justifiable, because the old classes will no longer exist. The "Call for Action" demands the emancipation of culture from the most primary schools right up to the universities. We do not demand this on behalf of any individual organization, but instead we demand a reformation so comprehensive that, by the time these children have completed school, something other than a unified school will exist.

Objections to such things are merely conservative prejudice, but we can go beyond that. We must recognize that culture has to be emancipated. We must free it on its own foundations, so that it no longer serves the state or marketplace but everything human consciousness can produce within culture. Thus, culture will no longer exist for only one class, but equally for all human beings.

Each morning you go to work in the factory and work until your work is finished.[3] After leaving the factory, perhaps you pass an educational institution established for certain people. Those institutes produce the people who, until now, have been the ruling class, leading the government and so on. Now, I ask: Do you honestly have any idea what goes on in those institutes? Do you know what is happening there? No! You know nothing at all. You can see this clearly in the separation of social classes; a gulf lies between them. The goal of the "Call to Action" is that everything done in the realm of culture should be accessible to everyone, and that people who work in the cultural realm should be responsible for all of humanity. You cannot achieve that if you do not free culture and make it independent. Consequently, Karl Marx's words about "surplus value" had such a deep affect upon the feelings of the proletariat.[4] In their heads, the proletariat did not understand that consciously, but they felt it was right in their hearts. These heartfelt demands are now expressed in historically important current events.

Why have these demands been taken up so strongly? Why? Why is Walther Rathenau so nervous about "surplus value?" [5] He is nervous because, until now, workers have known nothing about surplus value except that it exists. The concept is used by groups of people who strictly separate themselves from everyone else. Do modern workers know that they work for what the world finds completely useless? Do workers realize that much of their work is unfruitful, and that it only allows the bourgeoisie to live in untold luxury culturally? Due to their lack of thought, most modern people do not understand properly the relationship between the economic value of work and culture. It is culture that must lead humanity.

I want to give you an example that you may find somewhat amusing. Imagine a student who is to graduate from the university. As you know, there is an assignment to write a doctoral thesis, say, about the use of parentheses by Homer. In fact, Homer used no parentheses. Nevertheless, this student is supposed to write something about it. The student may need a year and a half and may actually do exemplary work on Homer's use of parentheses—at least according to modern educational and scientific standards. Now, however, we come to the relationship between this work on a doctoral thesis and the economy. When the thesis is completed, it will be printed and placed on a shelf in a library. One more thesis. No one looks at it, often not even the writer. From a practical perspective, however, that young student needs food, clothing, and money. Today, however, having money means utilizing the work of numerous people, and thus the proletariat must work for this doctoral thesis. They work for something in which they have no part. This is a ludicrous and rather comical example of something that happens innumerable times—not just hundreds, but maybe thousands of times.

You may ask: What kind of people lead us culturally? The reply is: They are those who graduate from the educational institutes that we ourselves are not allowed to attend. That situation will change when our culture is emancipated. It will change when economics and corporations no longer support those active in cultural life, and when the state no longer supports culture. It will change when those who are active in cultural life recognize daily that what they accomplish has value for humanity because human beings trust it. Culture must be based on trust between humanity and cultural leaders.

Some may complain that people today, even when talented, are not always recognized; talents, even genius, remain unrecognized. If we base such recognition on trust, how will that appear in the future? In the future, no one could make that objection, because the way people conduct themselves privately is just that, a private affair. What we are speaking of here is the relationship between culture and society. That relationship needs to be as I have described it. Culture must be independent. Culture has become what it is simply because it came to depend on state and economic interests during the last few centuries. This is why only those who speak as I mentioned yesterday could arise from culture, those we have entrusted to lead humanity.

Let's look at those who stood at the helm at the beginning of the World War. The foreign minister told the deep thinkers of Germany's parliament (who certainly should have understood something about the world situation) that the process of appeasement between countries was enjoying considerable progress. The foreign minister said we had an excellent relationship with Russia and that the cabinet in Petersburg was not listening to rabble-rousers in the press. He said that our friendly relationship with Russia was moving along favorably. He also said we were having positive discussions with England, which would probably result soon in world peace, and that the two governments were working toward a closer relationship.

The foreign minister said all of this in May, 1914! That is practical intelligence—the level of insight into the world situation that culture has wandered into over the last few centuries. We have wonderful scientists, because people have been well trained in science. This, however, is the point. We need cultural development that awakens the heart and soul to *life*. The point is, people must come to recognize life, so that in May 1914 no one could have claimed "world peace is secured," and the following August, something would not have happened that led to the deaths of ten or twelve million people and disabled three times as many. That must occur in cultural development. And it can occur only when culture is freed so that people do not just repeat facts and definitions about all sorts of things, but can also become practical.

When people in a free culture have practical intelligence, they know how to direct a company or guide the economy. Under such leadership, workers no longer feel the need to fight the director. Instead, workers would say that it is good to have a director who has something upstairs, so that the fruits of their own work can be maximized. Workers might say that, with a stupid director, they would have to work longer, but with a smart director working hours can be shortened without reducing their standard of living. Whether or not we work only a short time is not important. What is important is that if we work a shorter time, groceries and housing are still affordable. If we want to achieve something new, we must begin with the whole, and then address individual aspects. This is why I strongly emphasize that it is essential to begin by changing culture, that we must place it on a sound, independent foundation.

People have asked for a long time what the state should do. Now you see that, over the course of the past three or four centuries, the state has become a kind of god for the ruling classes. Others have echoed this same idea. Much of what was said about the state during this last terrible war reminds me of a discussion between Faust and the sixteen-year-old Gretchen. About God, Faust asks, "Does not the All-Embracing, the Preserver of All Things, embrace and preserve you and me and even Himself?" Today, or only recently, many company owners surely could have taught their workers about the state by asking:

Doesn't the state embrace you and me and even itself? The owner, however, would have thought: but especially me.

You see, this is precisely what we must recognize about glorifying the state. Out of practical necessity, the middle-class population has largely and quickly fled such glorification. If the state is no longer the great protector of industry, enthusiasm for it within those circles will cease. However, the proletariat must also be clear that it cannot treat the state as a god. Of course, people do not call the state "God," but they certainly consider it equally high.

People use the framework of state to direct the economy. This is healthy, however, only if the economy is not integrated into the state, and the state consists only of politics, or legal rights. Then, the state has its own foundation and is justified. Furthermore, we must also give economics its own foundation, because it must be administered in a completely different way than the state. We can achieve a healthy foundation for the social organism only when we attempt to achieve a threefold system. On the one side, we have culture, which must justify itself. It has no reason to exist unless those who create something cultural can justify that creation to humanity daily. In the center, we have legal rights, which must be democratic—or as democratic as possible. Here, we must consider everyone equally. We may discuss only what places one person equally beside another. Consequently, we must separate the state, since here we may not discuss whether one person's abilities are greater than those of another. This must all be separated from the state.

The state may consider only those issues involving human equality. Where, then, are all people equal? Today, I can give only two examples: *possession* and *work*. Let's begin with work. Marx's term *work as commodity* has entered deeply into the feelings of the proletarians. Why? Because, although they may not be able to define this intellectually, they nevertheless *feel* its meaning. Marx meant that the workers' *ability* to work is a commodity. Just as commodities are sold in the marketplace according to supply and demand, so also you sell your work in the work marketplace and receive only as much as the current economy will pay.

People have recently begun to believe various assurances of an improved future. But this will not be the result of anything done by the bourgeoisie, who have been living entirely without thought. We don't wish to condemn them completely, however, because they have accomplished one thing: statistical research. The English government during the 1840s—at the dawn of the social movement—provided an example of this. What did their research show? It was connected primarily with the English mines, and their research showed that down in the English mines (and this concerns an improvement, but one certainly not due to bourgeoisie efforts), there are boys and girls of nine, ten, and eleven working. Consequently, those children never saw the light of day, except on Sunday. Their working hours were so long that they went down the shaft before sunrise and returned only after sunset. This research recorded that down in the mines, half-naked pregnant women often worked with naked men. Above, however, in rooms well-heated with coal, people talked about brotherly love and charity, and of how all people wish to love one another. Researchers discovered these things, but people really learned nothing. These things did not cause any reflection. We don't need to point fingers at anyone, but where the bourgeois class actually went wrong—where they go wrong every time—was in their failure to act properly at the right time.

In the feelings of the proletariat, the idea has arisen that during ancient times there were slaves, and the whole person was sold. That person became the property of the owner, just like a cow. Later, when there were serfs, many human beings were sold, though somewhat fewer. More recently, only the capacity to work is sold. Nevertheless, when a worker sells the capacity for work, he or she must still accompany that capacity and work where it is sold. Workers must enter the factory, and thus sell themselves along with their capacity to work. Workers cannot simply send their working capacity to the factory. Thus, there is not much behind a work contract. We can expect an improvement only when the control of working capacity is separated from economics—that is, when the state, based on democratic principles, determines the quantity and methods of work used to accomplish a task. Thus, even before a worker enters the factory or workshop, the state has determined his or her work, and the state has heard the worker's voice in the matter through democratic principles.

What can we achieve through this? Well, on the one hand, economics depends on natural forces that can be mastered only to a certain extent. Such forces affect human conditions. It is predetermined how well wheat grows in a certain area, for example, or how many minerals lie beneath the Earth's surface, and we must adapt to it. We cannot specify a selling price that contradicts the availability of raw materials. That is one limitation. The other concerns the utilization of the human capacity to work. The natural forces necessary for growing wheat lie in the Earth, and the people dealing with economics cannot do anything about that. Similarly, the capacity to work must be added to the economy from outside. If that capacity is provided from within the economy, then wages will always depend on the level of economic activity. Thus, the worker can go to work and retain the rights to his or her work only when the type and amount of work is determined from outside the economic sector, with complete independence and based on purely democratic principles.

One's rights, pertaining to work, then become like a natural force. Economics is then caught between nature and the state, and what people found in the state during the last three or four centuries, the worker no longer finds. The worker no longer finds class struggle and class privilege. The worker then finds only human rights. This is the only way we can arrive at fruitful social progress. Only when we separate the state from the other two areas as a particular social form, do we find any degree of health in the way necessary for everyone on Earth. We must move beyond the bias that says economics should control the state, rather than having an independent state that controls economics; otherwise we will always think with the wrong orientation toward the future.

What I just said about labor rights is just as true of ownership rights. The modern basis of all ownership goes back to ancient conquests, the results of wars. But, everything became distorted. From an economic perspective, the concept of ownership makes no sense; it is a pure illusion. The concept of ownership merely has a calming effect on middle-class feelings. From an economic perspective, what does the concept of ownership mean? It is simply a right—the right to determine how things, land, or the means of production are used. Just as labor rights must be placed within the competency of the state, so also must the rights to dispose of property. This is possible only when you remove all economic and cultural power from the state. And this is possible only when both the economy and culture are completely independent, with only democracy left to the state.

At first it will be difficult for people to accept these ideas, but I am convinced that the proletariat will feel that they hold the future. The only movement within the economy would involve commodities, whereas, today, possession is also transferred, which is actually a right. Today, people can simply buy rights. With the purchase of work capacity, the purchaser also obtains a right over the person. By purchasing ownership of the means of production or by purchasing land, the purchaser also obtains the right of control. People purchase rights. In the future, people will no longer be able to purchase rights. The state should administer such rights, because it is not connected with buying and selling. This would allow every individual equal participation in the administration of these rights. Within the economy, nothing can circulate other than the production of commodities, their trading and consumption.

All of this occurs through consumption, and consequently, we must base the entire future economy on associative principles; we must base it on coalitions that arise from various professions; but mostly, we must base it on the needs of consumption. Today, we begin by simply producing, and, because we actually begin with the creation of wealth, that leads continually to crises that cause massive social suffering. If we begin with consumption, on the other hand, we give economic life a healthy foundation.

Yesterday, I gave an example of how people try somewhat clumsily to proceed in cultural production, so that they do not depend on the unfruitful work I described earlier. I would like to speak of that now. For many people, perhaps our society is still atrocious. But in the area of cultural production, our society has at least made an attempt involving something we could extend into other areas. About twenty years ago, I started writing books. I did not begin my work, however, as many of my contemporaries did. You know, of course, that many books are written; but only a few are read. These days, it is difficult to find enough time to read everything that is written. Economically, such book production is total nonsense. Imagine a book is written (this happens in thousands of cases), and during that time the author must eat. There are a certain number of typesetters who set the type, the paper must be produced, and so many bookbinders will then bind the book. Finally, the book appears in, say, a thousand copies. But, perhaps, only fifty sell, and the other 950 copies are ground into paper pulp. What actually happened?

We need to look at reality. In this case, a certain number of people worked on the book, and have worked free of charge for the person who wrote the book. From this, you can see how much suffering today is based on unproductive and useless work, thrown to the wind.

What have we done in our Anthroposophical Society? I started a publishing house, because there is nothing we can do about the ordinary book trade, which is completely integrated into the modern economy. We never printed a book before there were enough people interested in purchasing every copy—that is, before there was an actual need for the book. You can achieve that through work, and you have to draw people's attention to things, but not, of course, through some billboard advertising, like "Magi's Excellent Soup Bouillon." Advertising can make people aware of an item, but we must begin with needs determined by consumption. That can occur, however, only when there are consumer cooperatives, and when those cooperatives have an economic basis. It is unnecessary to integrate them into politics when we have democracy. That, however, is something today's proletariat does not see and cannot easily imagine at present.

Now (since I want to speak with you honestly) I can certainly bring up one more question to show how the proletariat, through its own fate, experiences the terrible things that have arisen through the integration of economics with the state. Since the state still does not exist upon its own sound foundation—that is, democracy, independent of the needs of the economy—what do countless proletarians see as the only salvation during economically difficult times? Some might say that we must end strikes so that the proletariat can participate in a general, independent culture. The state must take a position between the economy and culture, and it must stand on its own democratic foundation.

Today, all of these things combine and mix together because of middle-class interests in past centuries, and they were combined even more strongly during the first two decades of the twentieth century. Today, when the facts speak so loudly, we see the final goal of many proletarians. What is the final justifiable goal you struggle so hard for? I need to say only one word to touch what countless proletarians think but cannot yet properly feel, because they cannot foresee the total economic consequences. I need say only the word *strike*. I realize, of course, that if all proletarians could make progress without strikes, they would reject every strike. I cannot imagine, in any case, that any reasonable proletarian would want to strike merely for the sake of going on strike.

Why do proletarians strike so often today? Simply because the economy and the state have merged. The strike is purely an economic tool and only effects the economy. But its use is often intended to force a legal and political change. The reason can exist only in the unhealthy state of our society, where there is no separation between the state and the economy. Those who look at the economy know it can be healthy only when production is not limited, but strikes limit production. Those who believe they must strike, act because the state and the economy are combined.

It is a great misfortune today that what should be divided into three parts is integrated. It forces us to destroy life. There is no way to finally end all strikes, other than giving the state its own economic foundation. This would make it impossible to gain rights through economics. I know that when people realize this, they will say that, if people finally become reasonable and tell us they are ready to take up what will fulfill social necessity, we will no longer strike. We know we cannot achieve some things immediately. We are willing to wait, but we would prefer some guarantee.

During the war, in an attempt to find some way out of that terrible misery, I spoke to a number of so-called authorities and presented them with the "Call to Action." Some important leaders have long had that "Call." I told them that what I presented did not just come out of my head; I am no more clever or intelligent than anyone else. But I have observed life, and it has shown me that, in the next twenty years, we should direct all our efforts toward achieving this threefold division—not as a program, but as a human necessity. I told them they had a choice: they could either be reasonable and make this a counterproposal to Wilson's "Fourteen Points," or, if we cannot help ourselves, Wilson will not be able to help us either. They could choose to use the "Call" as the basis of an international policy and propose what should happen when peace is achieved. I told them they had the choice between taking up reason and facing revolution and catastrophe. Those people did not use reason, and I ask you: Did the second possibility occur or not? That is a question we must ask today.

What worries people today so much is that, in general, there is still that old lack of thought, and it has not been replaced by truly fruitful and practical ideas. The threefold idea is genuinely practical for life, and consequently, I am convinced that it will happen. We will experience it if there is some possibility that the proletariat recognizes its value. We need to force ourselves to progress socially in this way. Then, all the unproductive social desires will cease. We will base our work on reason that arises from the proletarian feeling about other ways that have not worked reasonably. That is what is important.

I could have remained silent and refrained from speaking about strikes, but I wanted to show you that I am always willing to speak out about my convictions. This perhaps gives me a

right to say that, although much of what I have said contradicts
your own views, you should not doubt my honest intention to
genuinely achieve what the proletariat must also achieve.

For over a century, the words *liberty, equality, fraternity* have
called throughout humankind. During the nineteenth century,
many intelligent people wrote that those three words are contradictory. And they were right. Why? Because people were hypno-
tized by the idea of a unified state. Only when we understand
these three words, or impulses, as cultural liberty, democratic
equality, and community love through economic association,
can they become truly significant. In the twentieth century we
must fulfill the ideal that was still incomprehensible at the end of
the eighteenth century, but nevertheless coursed through
humanity. We want genuine equality, fraternity, and freedom,
but we must first understand how necessary it is to separate the
social organism into three parts. When we see how necessary that
is, and when we can hope to awaken an understanding for these
three aspects within the proletariat, then we can also express conviction. I believe that a more or less unconscious, healthy, and
progressive idea exists within the modern proletarian movement.
The modern proletariat has become class conscious. Behind that
is a consciousness of humanity—a consciousness that we must
achieve human dignity. Through life itself, in a manner worthy
of humanity, the proletariat attempts to answer the questions:
What am I as a human being? Do I exist within human society as
a worthy human being? If the proletariat achieves a social organization that can answer these questions with, "Yes," then, today's
demands will be resolved through a sound social organism.
Workers will accomplish what they have set out to do, and they
will free the proletariat from poverty and despair. They will also
achieve freedom for all of humanity—they will free everything
that is human, everything that deserves real freedom in the
human being.

THE SOCIAL BASIS OF
PUBLIC EDUCATION
1

THE BASIS OF WHAT I HAVE TO SAY today about primary education can serve us in these serious times. I believe you will have realized that what I could only hint at in my book *Towards Social Renewal*[1] implies many things about the basis and facts of the new world situation. What I must say about this subject today, particularly whatever suggestions I can make, I can only say in the form of some guidelines, not in an exhaustive discussion.

If we look at our modern situation—and we must do this to understand these times—the cleft between what we might call a declining society and a rising, but as yet chaotic, society is readily apparent. Today, I want to make you aware of only a specific problem, and ask you to consider this problem in conjunction with this series of lectures as a whole.

I wish to begin by pointing out the obvious fact that our society, primarily sustained by the middle class, is in the process of rapid decline. It is equally obvious that another society is beginning to dawn, and, as I have mentioned before, for a number of yet uncomprehended reasons, it is one borne by the working class. If you want to understand these things—you can still feel them, but they remain unclear—you must comprehend their symptoms. Symptoms are, of course, always anecdotal, and I ask that today you take this into account as you listen to my observations. The topic itself forces me to pull the particulars out of context, but I will attempt to present these symptoms so that they are not inflammatory or demagogic, but rather so that they arise out of the situation itself. It is so easy to be misunderstood today, but we must take this chance anyway.

Over the past years, I have often pointed out the fact that the basis of our world view allows us to be true proponents and defenders of the modern scientific viewpoint. You know how often I have brought up everything we can say in defense of the scientific point of view. However, I have never neglected to mention the dreadful shadow side of this viewpoint. I recently made note of how visible this is when we look at individual cases in what we might call a symptomatological manner, that is, if we look at things empirically. I gave high praise in a different connection to a wonderful modern work by Oskar Hertwig,[2] a particularly good book on biology, *The Development of Organisms: A Refutation of Darwin's Theory.* To avoid misunderstandings following the publication of Hertwig's second small volume, I also said that after this man had produced such a marvelous scientific work, he then wrote a quite inferior book about his observations of social life. This is a significant fact. It indicates that what is necessary for an understanding of the present, namely, an understanding of the social impulses of our times, cannot be built upon even such a marvelous foundation as the basis of the scientific point of view.

Today, I want to mention another example whereby you can easily see how middle class education, on the one hand, heads toward its demise and can be saved only in a particular way, and how something is arising, on the other hand, that we must appropriately preserve and protect with understanding so that it can be the beginning of future society.

I have a book here that appeared just after the end of the war, entitled rather pompously, *The Beacon, World View and Way of Life.*[3] It is so symptomatic and is such a typical product of the declining middle class. This "beacon" is best suited for throwing considerable darkness upon everything connected with what social development and its spiritual basis now need. A curious group came together to write strange essays about the so-called reconstruction of our social organism. I can mention only a few passages from this voluminous book. There is, for instance, Jakob von Uexküll, a scientist, a truly good, typical scientist, and this is important. He is not only knowledgeable about science, but also, as a scientist, is completely a man of the present. However, he feels it his duty, as do others with a scientific background, to turn his attention toward social reform. He has learned about the "cell state," as scientific circles often call organisms. He certainly learned to develop his mind, and with this developed mind he now looks at social life. I want to mention only a few specific points so that you can see how this person, not scientifically, but in a quite proper scientific way of thinking directed toward practical life, arrives at totally absurd observations of modern society. He turns his attention first to the social organism, then to the biological organism, and sees how illness can disturb the harmony of a biological organism. He then says the following about the social organism: Illness can disturb the harmony within the organism. We call the most terrible form of illness in the human body, "cancer." It is characterized by a boundless activity of protoplasm no longer concerned with the maintenance of the body, but simply the creation of free protoplasm cells. These displace the normal structure of the body but in themselves can do nothing useful since they are without structure. We see the same illness in human society when the proletarian slogan "Liberty, Equality, and Fraternity" replaces the state-oriented slogan "Coercion, Inequality, and Subordination."

Here you have a typical scientific thinker. He considers it a cancer on the body politic when the popular impulse arises for "Liberty, Equality and Fraternity." He wants to have coercion instead of liberty, inequality instead of equality, and subordination instead of fraternity. What he has learned about the organization of cells he now applies to the social organism. His other observations are also important when considered symptomatologically. He finds something in the social organism corresponding to the circulatory system of biological organisms, but not in the way that I have described it in various lectures. He pictures it as the circulation of gold. Of this he says, "Gold can circulate independent of commodities and eventually arrives in the large banks acting as central depositories ('gold hearts')." Therefore, the scientist seeks something in the social organism corresponding to the heart and finds it in the large banks acting as depositories that "can have a major influence upon the total circulation of gold and commodities."

I want you to know that I am not intending to make fun of this. I would only like you to see how someone coming from this direction must think when he has the courage to think through to the final consequences. Due to the developments of the last three or four centuries, many modern people fool themselves into believing that this kind of thinking is comprehensible. That is because these people are asleep in their souls. They have succumbed to a kind of anesthetic, a social anesthetic that inhibits their seeing the content of middle-class education with wakeful souls. You see, I have shed some light upon this "beacon" through a symptom. I have shed some light upon the basis of modern education, insofar as it attempts to comprehend social life through scientific thinking. Through another example, I want to show you the effects of what we meet in the spiritual area.

Among those people whose articles are gathered in this book is someone more spiritually oriented, Friedrich Niebergall. Now, we can mention this Friedrich Niebergall because he sees some things we value in a positive manner. The problem, though, is *how* he arrives at his positive view. If you look at the *how* without egotism, but with concern for the dominant social trends, then his positive attitude will not particularly impress you. It is important not to fool yourselves about such things. We know, of course, or at least we should know, that the intent of our work in Anthroposophy has long been to create a spiritual foundation for the changes occurring today. Of course, here the most extreme things collide. I have experienced time and again how people taking part in our spiritual scientific efforts drift toward other things they feel to be quite "related." However, these things are quite different from our spiritual scientific efforts and actually represent the worst of decadent middle-class society, whereas spiritual science has always been completely at odds with this middle-class standpoint. Thus, we find with this Mr. Niebergall, for example, that someone who cannot even see these two streams totally mixes things together. In Mr. Niebergall's article, we find mention of Johannes Müller, someone who is simply characteristic of our decadent culture. On the very next page, we find my name. We even find things that I am attempting to do described ever so sweetly. You know, though, that I always intend my efforts concerning spiritual science to stimulate healthy human intellect and to fight, in the firmest manner, against all this nebulous mysticism, all this mystical theosophical stuff. This is only possible if we do not use today's scientific orientation, but the true thinking learned from science so that we can bring clear insight and ideas worthy of striving for into the highest realms of cognition.

After this man has mentioned how beautiful much of Anthroposophy is, he adds, "A muddled confusion of supposed facts about the life of the soul, humanity, and the cosmos, as were once found in the comprehensive descriptions of creation offering the secret wisdom of the East to a time similarly seeking depth and peace of soul, surrounds the practical basic truths of Anthroposophy." It is not possible to say anything less to the point than this. The writer designates this as "muddled confusion" only because he does not have the will to think about the mathematically exact methods of spiritual science. Most people who wish to use the decadent manner of thinking to gain an idea about such things do not have this will. The results of precisely disciplined inner experience then appear to such people as muddled confusion. However, this "muddled confusion," which makes possible the achievement of such mathematical clarity, perhaps even mathematical sobriety, is precisely what protects anthroposophical activity from those babbling mystics and foggy-minded Theosophy. Without this so-called muddled confusion we can gain nothing at all in the way of a proper foundation for future cultural life. Certainly, we have to struggle since, due to our present social conditions, we can pursue spiritual science only to a modest extent. We have to struggle because, as often occurs, most people who have time, in fact, nothing other than time, for spiritual scientific questions, have exactly these old, decaying habits of thinking and feeling. We have to struggle desperately with the sectarianism that so easily spreads among us and is, in truth, the opposite of what should actually occur. We need to struggle against all kinds of personality conflicts that lead as a matter of course to those personal attacks that have so rampantly shot up like weeds from the soil of the spiritual scientific movement.

Those who view modern cultural life while considering such symptoms as these can easily admit that innovations are necessary, particularly in the area of spiritual work. The call for a more social form of society sounds at a time when people are generally filled with antisocial desires and instincts. These antisocial desires and instincts are particularly visible in people's private lives. They are visible in how one person appreciates another, that is, actually, how they do not appreciate another. A major characteristic of modern people is the way they think past one another, talk past one another and go past one another. The instinctive capability to really want to understand people as we meet them, appears very rarely in our times. There is something else that accompanies this now rare social instinct, and that is the capacity of people to be convinced of something they are not connected to through social position or education or birth. Modern people have tremendous difficulty becoming excited about even the most beautiful new ideas. People think past the best things. This is a basic characteristic of our time. You know that I have recently spoken of factual logic, in contrast to merely intellectual logic, as being the most important thing for the present. A result of thinking past the best things is that modern people have no desire to actively work things through. Rather, they want to submit to authorities and emotions. The people who now speak so much about freedom from authority are actually those who most believe in authority and who most intensively seek authority. Because modern people are so asleep in their souls today, they seldom observe this. However, we can see an alarming characteristic among those standing in our declining society, unable to find a way out, namely, the desire to return to the lap of the Catholic Church. If people today knew of the underlying reasons for the desire to return to the Catholic Church, they would be very astonished. If this movement becomes more widespread, then under current conditions we will soon see great masses of people move into the lap of the Catholic Church. Those who have just a little capacity to observe the idiosyncrasies of our modern society know that such a fate threatens us.

Where are all these things coming from? I need to make you aware of a basic tendency of modern social life. A particular tendency has arisen in the last centuries and has taken on increasingly large dimensions. It will spread even further in those countries that remain civilized after the chaotic events of the present. I am referring to the particularly technical attitude that society has taken on in modern times. I have much more to say about this specific question than I can say now, and I will do it sometime in the future when I can go into all the details. Technical society has a very special characteristic, namely, it is, at its core, a thoroughly altruistic society. In other words, technology can spread in a human way only when the people active in technology develop altruism, the opposite of egotism. Every new wave of technology in society shows, for those who can observe such things, that in a technological society it becomes increasingly necessary to work without egotism. At the same time, something else developed from capitalism that is not necessarily connected with technical society, or at least, need not remain connected. Capitalism, as private capitalism, must act egotistically, since its nature is one of egotistical activity. In modern times, two diametrically opposed streams meet one another, namely, modern technology, which requires human beings free of egotism, and private capitalism, which arose in an older period and can flourish only when people accept egotistical desires. You can see that this has forced us into the present situation, and only a cultural life with the courage to break with old traditions can bring us out of it.

Many people today ask what a future-oriented public education, elementary and vocational, must be. When we consider the question of education, we must ask such people, if they intend to improve elementary education for everyone, how they can do so if they remain within the modern educational and cultural context. Do you have the material needed? What can you really do? From your standpoint which is, perhaps, socially well-intended, you might found schools for the general public, schools for continuing education. You could do all of this out of your goodwill. But, do you have the understanding necessary to do the things with your goodwill that are necessary for the good of the people? You tell us that you will create libraries, drama and music productions, exhibits, lecture series, and continuing education. We must also ask: Which books will you put in your libraries? What kind of science will you discuss in your lectures? You will put those books in your libraries that have been based upon the middle-class education now in decline. In your schools for continuing education, you will allow people who have received a middle-class education to lecture on science. You are reshaping the educational system, but into these new forms you toss everything you have taken from the old system. For example, you say that you have long striven to give a democratic form to public education. The states have, until now, refused this because they want to raise people as good servants of the state. Yes, you do not accept people being raised as good servants of the state, yet you allow these same servants of the state to educate people. This is because until now you have paid no attention to anything other than these servants of the state. Now you place their books in your libraries, you allow them to bring their scientific way of thinking to the public in lecture series, and you permit their entire manner of thinking to flood your schools of higher learning. You can see from this that we must take things up in a much deeper way in these serious times, much more deeply than they are currently taken up by one group or another.

To make something clear, we want to take a look at some details. We want to begin with what we can, for now, call an elementary school. By elementary school, I mean everything that people learn after they have outgrown family upbringing, when we add school to family as a place of upbringing and instruction. To those who understand human nature, formal education should clearly not become part of children's development until approximately the time after the child begins the change of teeth. This is just as much a law of science as other scientific laws. If, instead of acting according to fixed schemes, people would act according to the nature of the human being, then they would use the rule that children should begin formal education after the change of teeth.

The question is, what principles should we use as the foundation of education? Here we must recall that people who are really capable of thinking and moving with the dawning cultural development can do nothing other than accept what lies in human nature itself as the valid guideline for formal education. The basic principle of elementary education must lie in an understanding of human nature in the period between the change of teeth until puberty. From that and many other similar things, you can see that nothing can result other than a unified school for all people. That is obvious because the laws that play into human development between approximately the ages of seven and fourteen are the same for all people. The central question in education is: How far are we to bring children into being human beings by the time they are fourteen or fifteen years old? This alone is pedagogical thinking for elementary school. Only this is thinking about the nature of education in a truly modern sense. As a result, we cannot ignore the need to break with the old educational system in a fundamental and radical manner. Then we must begin in earnest to teach children according to human development during the period mentioned. To do this, we must create a certain foundation, one that, when social goodwill is present, is not some nebulous idea for the future, but one that we can immediately practice. Above all, we must create this foundation by completely transforming the testing and education of teachers. When we test teachers today, we often do so only to verify that they know something or, failing that, if they are a little bright, that they can look it up later in an encyclopedia or other reference. We could leave this completely out of the teaching examination, but then the major portion of the current teachers' examination would fall by the way. The question we must ask in today's examinations is whether this person, who will be responsible for the education of developing human beings, has an active personal relationship to children, whether he or she can develop a fruitful relationship to children. We need to ask if these future teachers can, with their entire "mentality," dive into the souls and the entire being of children. Then they will not be reading teachers or arithmetic teachers or drawing teachers and so forth; rather they will truly educate and develop children.

In the future, "examinations" will have to be different from those of today. We will need to discover if the teaching staff can actually develop and educate children. That means the teacher will know what to teach children if they are to learn to think. The teacher will know what to teach children if they are to develop their feeling (something closely related to memory, a fact that only a few people know today because most professors are very poor psychologists). The teacher must know what to teach children so that their wills develop from the seeds they accept between the ages of seven and fifteen, so that their wills remain strong throughout life. We can develop the will when we do all practical, bodily, and artistic exercises in a way that befits the developing nature of the human being. The teacher must meticulously direct his or her efforts toward developing the human being.

From this we can show how to use everything in conventional human culture, namely, language, reading and writing. In elementary school we can best use all this to develop the child's thinking. As strange as it may sound today, thinking is the most external thing in human beings, and we must develop it through those aspects that make us a part of the social organism. Recall for a moment that people are not born into the world with a capacity for reading and writing, but that this has its foundation in human community life. Thus, to develop thinking, a reasonable instruction in language must enter relatively early. Of course, we must not teach ancient languages, but, rather, languages spoken by modern civilized people with whom we live. Reasonable education in languages, not the grammatical nonsense taught in modern middle schools, must begin in the earliest grades.

It will be necessary to educate consciously in a way that affects the feeling and the memory connected with it. Although everything related to arithmetic, algebra, and geometry[4] exists between thinking and feeling, everything received through memory affects feeling alone, for example, everything that we teach in history, or what we teach through the telling of stories. I can mention only a few things now. Children can take in an extraordinary amount if we teach it properly.

We must also give particular attention to cultivating the will through physical and artistic exercises during these years. In this area, we will need quite new things. We have already made a beginning with what we call eurythmy. In physical education today you see much that is decadent and in decline, but it pleases many people. We want to add[5] something to it that, when taught to children, becomes ensouled physical education instead of merely physical exercise. Until now, we have had the opportunity to show this only to the workers at the Waldorf-Astoria factory, through the sympathetic support of Mr. Molt.[6] However, eurythmy can create a kind of willing that remains with the child throughout life, whereas all other physical education has the peculiarity that it becomes diminished during life due to various events and experiences. It is particularly important to proceed rationally here. We will also create connections that no one in modern instruction thinks of, for example, between drawing and geography. It is tremendously important for developing human beings that they receive a truly meaningful education in drawing. The teacher would guide the student into, for instance, drawing the globe from differing perspectives, into drawing the mountains and rivers, and then, further, into drawing astronomical subjects, the planetary system and so forth. We will, of course, have to do this at the proper time, and not, for example, begin with the seven-year-old child. However, when we teach geographic drawing in the proper manner, from perhaps the age of twelve on, by the time the child reaches fourteen or fifteen, such drawing is not only possible, but also something tremendously beneficial for the developing child. To develop feeling and memory, we must develop a living picture of nature in even the youngest people. You know how often I have spoken of a living picture of nature. I have summarized numerous points of view by saying that, unfortunately, there are many people living in cities who cannot tell the difference between wheat and rye in the fields. The names of the grains are not important; what is important is to see the relationships between things. For those who understand human nature, it is overwhelming to see what people lose when they do not learn to differentiate at the proper time. The development of human capacities must always occur at the proper time. It is difficult to see (I am speaking only symptomatologically) that people have not learned to differentiate between wheat and rye. I am referring to something that, of course, encompasses a great deal.

What I have just discussed from a pedagogical standpoint concerning instruction in elementary school has a specific consequence in terms of factual logic. This consequence is that we may use nothing in instruction that the child cannot retain in one form or another for the remainder of life. But today, people normally take only accomplishments into account. Today, learning to read results only in an ability to read, learning arithmetic results only in an ability to do arithmetic. However, if you think about the relationship of modern learning to feeling and memory, you will see that children learn an enormous amount, only to forget it and to no longer have it later in life. The particular distinction of education in the future will be that everything presented to children will remain with the adult for his or her whole life.

Now we come to the question of what to do with people when they have completed the unified school and go on into further life. In this case they must overcome everything education contains of the unhealthiness of the old cultural life that has caused such a terrible gulf between classes of people.

The Greeks and Romans were educated out of the life of their times and were thus able to connect their education with their lives. In our time, though, there is nothing that connects the important years spent in school with the quite different life afterward. Many people who come into a position of leadership have learned what the Greeks and Romans learned and are therefore divorced from life. Education today is spiritually inefficient. We have now come to a point in human development, only people do not know it, when, to preserve our relationship to those times, it is absolutely unnecessary to educate people as in ancient times. For some time now, education has so incorporated what people generally need from ancient civilizations that we can gain it without training for many years in a foreign atmosphere. We can attain what we need from the Greeks and Romans, as has been done in recent times, but that is something for academics and has nothing to do with general social education. The work of the past has completed what general social education needs from ancient civilizations. If we just learn properly what is available, we no longer need to learn Greek and Latin to understand these old civilizations. Greek and Latin are not at all necessary, and they are not at all helpful in important things. I need only remind you that I found it necessary to say, to avoid grave misunderstandings, that although Mr. Wilamowitz[7] is certainly a good Greek scholar, he had translated the Greek dramas in a horrible, in a terrible way. The academic journals, of course, stood in awe of these translations.

We will need to learn to allow children to be active in life during their school years. When we create an education whereby children can be active in life in their early years and when, at the same time, we become able to educate efficiently, then we can give children a truly living education. This will enable those with a tendency toward handwork to also begin a lifelong development after the age of fourteen. We must create the possibility also for those who turn to handwork at an early age to participate in what leads to an understanding of life. In the future, we may not teach anything to people under the age of twenty-one that comes as a result of recent research. Until then, teaching may include only what has already reached maturity. We can then go to work with enormous efficiency. We need only understand what pedagogical efficiency means. Of course, we cannot be lazy if we want to work efficiently in pedagogy. I have often mentioned my personal experiences. I was once given a weak-minded eleven-year-old child to teach.[8] Through pedagogical efficiency, within two years I brought that child to a point where he had learned everything he had missed before the age of eleven when he could really do nothing at all. This was possible only because I could take into account both his physical and his soul needs so that I could teach in the most efficient manner thinkable. I often achieved this by preparing for three hours to teach him something in a half-hour, or even a quarter-hour that would otherwise have taken several hours because of his situation. From a social standpoint, I can also mention that I had to do all this for a single boy while teaching three other children in a much different way. Remember, though, that if we had a truly social manner of educating, then we could take care of a whole group of such people. It makes no difference whether you need to handle one or forty children in this efficient manner. I would not complain about the number of students in a class, but this lack of complaining is directly connected with the principle of efficiency in teaching. The only thing is, you must know that until the age of fourteen, children do not form judgments, and that if you require them to form judgments, you destroy their brains. It is pedagogical nonsense to use modern calculators to replace the memorization of arithmetic with judgment; this destroys the human brain and makes it decadent. We can only develop human judgment after the age of fourteen. Then the teacher must introduce things that appeal to judgment. Then, we can introduce all those things that, for example, relate to a logical understanding of reality. When the day comes in the higher grades when the cabinetmaker or machinist's apprentice sits in class with someone who will, perhaps, become a teacher, you will see something that, although it has elements of specialization, is still a unified school. In this kind of unified school, everything that needs to be together in life will be together. If that is not so, then we will move even further into social illness than we already are. An understanding of life must inspire all teaching. We need to rationally and efficiently teach students from fifteen to twenty years of age, everything having to do with agriculture, commerce, industry, and trade. No one should pass through this period without acquiring at least an idea of what occurs in agriculture, in trade, industry, or commerce. These things need to become individual disciplines and are much more necessary than much of the rubbish that now fills education during these years.

At this time in life, we need to teach all those things I would generally call world affairs. Among these are history and geography and everything connected with an understanding of nature, but always as they relate to the human being, so that children learn about human beings in a universal context.

Among the people taught in this way will be those who, due to other social circumstances, will become intellectual workers, educated in all possible fields at the special academic schools. The education in these modern specialized institutions is terribly inefficient. I know many people will not admit this, but these schools are very inefficient, and they validate the most curious things of the now-declining world view. I experienced it myself when people became excited about replacing lectures with seminars in the areas of literature and history at the university. We still hear demands today that lectures should be only a minor part of the instruction, and that we should do much more as seminars. You know these seminars; there the real disciples of the professors come together to learn strictly according to the directions of the professor and, as is said, to work scientifically. They do their work there and become "trained to perform intellectually." We have all experienced the result of this "training for intellectual performance." It always tends toward a mental stiffness.

It is something quite different if people, during this period of life when they move toward specialized education, freely hear reasonable lecturers and then have the opportunity to freely discuss them. Of course, we can also do practical exercises in conjunction with this, but the nonsense concerning seminars must stop. This is simply an undesirable result of the late-nineteenth-century tendency toward drilling and away from a free development of the human being.

Of course, when we speak of education, we must emphasize that there must be a certain basic education that is the same for everyone. Whether I become a physician, a lawyer, or a secondary or elementary school teacher is one matter; however, everyone must receive the same general education. Someone who later works in a trade must have the opportunity to have the same general education as someone who will become a physician, engineer, architect, or chemist. Modern people seldom take this into account, but there are many things in some higher schools that are better than they were earlier. When I was a student in Vienna at the technical college, there was one professor who gave lectures on general history. After the fourth or fifth lecture he stopped because there were no more students attending. There was also one professor of literature at that college. These were the means used then to provide some general education along with what was specific to a given field. There were also exercises in speaking, that is, in lecturing, like those given by Uhland in his lectures about literature, but I always had to sneak someone else in because he would give them only if two students were there. I could keep them going only if I brought someone else in, and that was almost always a different person. Apart from that, only the lectures about politics or statistics contained what students needed for general life. As I said, things have gotten better, but the driving force for our whole social life is still not better. It will become better, however, when we create a possibility to present everything needed for a general human education in a way that is generally understandable. We must not present these things in ways that only those with specialized training can understand. People have often surprised me when they complained about my lectures on Anthroposophy. If they had a more positive attitude, they might have said that the part concerning Anthroposophy is not so important, but what I say about scientific things, which would normally receive high praise if a natural scientist presented them, is sufficient. You all know that my lectures are filled with popularized scientific knowledge. Unfortunately, many people do not see the positive, but complain about the negative. People do not want precisely what is suitable for inclusion in general human knowledge, so that the average person can understand it as well as the academic. This is due to the kind of thinking and the entire treatment it incorporates, including, for example, what we need to present about the natural sciences. With this presentation, people can generally understand natural science. Look at the other developments in world views. Do you believe, for example, that monists[9] could understand each other if they did not have a general understanding of natural science? No, without such a basis, they would only be chattering. What we do here as Anthroposophy can transform natural and historical knowledge into something everyone can understand. Think for a moment how easily everyone could understand my development of the great historical change in the middle of the fifteenth century. I think everyone could probably understand it. But, without this foundation, no one can really understand anything of the present social movement. People do not understand the social movement because they do not know how humanity has developed since the middle of the fifteenth century. If I develop such things, then people come along and say that nature makes no leaps, and that I am incorrect when I presume there to be such a leap in development in the fifteenth century. Someone always brings up the idiotic sentence, "Nature makes no leaps." Nature continually makes leaps, the leap from the green leaf to the quite differently formed sepal and the leap from sepal to the flower petal. The development of human life is the same. Those who do not teach the nonsensical lies of conventional history, but teach what really occurred, know that the more subtle elements of the human constitution are now much different than they were in the middle of the fifteenth century. What is happening now is a continuation of something that has gripped humanity at its core since that time. If we want to understand the modern social movement, we must recognize such laws of historical development.

You need only recall how I do things here, and you can acknowledge that no one needs any special knowledge, nor do they need to be well educated in the older sense to understand it. Everyone can understand it. The future demands that we do not develop philosophies or world views that only those who have gone through a specific class-oriented education can understand. Take a look at something philosophical, for instance from Eucken[10] or Paulsen[11] or anything else from which you would want to teach, or any academic psychology text. If you look at these horror stories, you will soon lay them aside because without professional training no one can understand even the language used. We can achieve a general education only if we fundamentally reform the educational system in the sense I have attempted to describe today.

You see, we can also say for this area that the great day of reckoning has arrived, not just a small one. Our goal in teaching and education must be to develop social motives, or perhaps, better said, social instincts, so that people no longer simply pass by their fellow human beings. Today, the teachers pass by the students and the students pass by the teachers. In the future, people will understand one another so that a living and lively relationship will develop. This can only occur, though, if we once and for all put an end to the old ways. This *can* be done. From the facts of the matter, it is not at all impossible. That it seems impossible is only a reflection of our prejudices. People cannot imagine the possibility of doing things differently than they have been done until now. People have a gigantic fear that they might lose their traditions, particularly in the area of spiritual life. They have no idea how great this fear is, but of course, they do not have a complete overview of things. For example, people cannot comprehend what we can achieve through efficient teaching. As I have often said, if we choose the proper time in life, we can teach people from the beginning of geometry, that is, lines and angles, all the way up to the Pythagorean theorem in only three or four hours. You should see children's joy when they suddenly have an understanding of the Pythagorean theorem after only three or four hours of teaching. But, just remember how much nonsense takes place in modern teaching before this theorem is arrived at. We waste so very much mental work, and that becomes visible in later life, it radiates out of all of life and into the most practical areas. Today, people must decide to fundamentally rethink all these things. Otherwise we will only sink deeper into decline, never finding the ascending path.

THE SOCIAL BASIS OF
PUBLIC EDUCATION

2

STUTTGART, MAY 18, 1919

I DO NOT INTEND to continue last Sunday's discussion in the normal way. Then I did my best in a preliminary sketch to present how to think about culture and teaching independent of the life of the state and the economy. I tried to show that if there is such a separation, teachers would need to use the various subjects to form a kind of anthropological pedagogy, or perhaps I should say, a kind of anthropological teaching. I then noted that a significant goal for the future is to change the education and certification of teachers, so that we can determine whether a given person is suitable for teaching.

I want to set aside further discussion of pedagogical questions until a later time. Today, I want to try to continue my main topic in a very different way. I want to show you how I think we need to speak today, to serve the needs of our time when we present impulses of modern development at education conferences or such. If we wish to move out of confusion and chaos in the present, we really must speak very differently about things than people imagine.

At teachers' conferences, as I can show you through some examples, people speak in the old time-tested manner. We can achieve a truly free education for the future only when teachers are raised to that level where they have an overview of the great tasks of the present time and their consequences for the educational system. Certainly, I do not present the way I am speaking as being necessary or even exemplary. I want only to indicate the direction in which to speak to modern teachers to inspire them to work toward a free education. They must come to understand the great and comprehensive tasks of the present. Teachers must have insight into the forces hidden in modern history. They must know of the impulses arising out of the past that we must now end. They must understand the impulses arising from modern life that require particular care and attention. We must provide, in the best sense, we might say the most ideal sense, a sociopolitical standpoint that can form the basis of the inspiration teachers need. People must understand, for example, that our current pedagogy is at all levels of education completely bankrupt, and they must see the reasons for this. Modern pedagogy has lost its direct connection with life. Today pedagogues speak about all kinds of methodological questions and of the benefits of allowing the state to direct education. They would probably speak of such benefits almost automatically even if they had a theoretical understanding of the necessity of the threefold social organism. At no other time have self-perpetuating thinking habits been as strong as in the present. These habits are particularly evident in the development of pedagogical ideas. Pedagogical ideas have suffered under something we cannot escape in modern times, but must, in fact, escape. There are questions today that we can no longer answer with the reply that, "Judging from experience, this or that may be possible." In such cases, hesitation arises in human hearts and souls. Today, we must answer numerous questions with the question, "If we want to escape our present confusion and chaos, does not this or that have to occur?" Here we are dealing with a question of will and need not allow the often justifiable intellectual hesitation based on

so-called experience. Experience has value only after the will
has properly processed it. Experience abounds today, but the
will has properly processed only a little of it. From a strictly
intellectual perspective, we can say little against much that people say in the field of pedagogy today, and it is actually quite
wise from this perspective. Today, though, it is important to see
the real problem, namely, that our pedagogy has become
divorced from life.

Allow me to make a personal remark here. About twenty-
three years ago a society for college education was formed in
Berlin. The head of this society was the astronomer Wilhelm
Förster,[1] and I also belonged to it. We held a series of lectures
for the society. Most of these lectures would lead you to believe
that you need know only certain formal things about the treatment of the different sciences or the composition of the different faculties or similar things. I attempted, but without much
success, to make clear that a college only represents a cross section of general life. I said that if we want to speak about college
pedagogy, we must begin with the questions: "Where do the
various areas of study lie in relation to life in general? What
impulses from the various realms of life do we need to observe,
so that real life will enter the college and make the college representative of life in general?" If you do not think about such
things abstractly, but instead look at them concretely, then you
can see many ways to view things such as limiting the amount
of time devoted to one or another subject, or how we can
approach one or another subject. The moment modern pedagogy attempts to look at such limitations, everything fails, and
colleges become nothing other than places to drill people,
divorced from the world.

What are the intrinsic reasons, the deep inner reasons, why
everything has become the way it is? The magnificent recent
development of scientific thinking has led to a comprehension

of the human being as a strictly natural being, at the same time cutting off any true understanding of humanity, that understanding of humanity that we recently spoke of as being the essential basis of real pedagogy. Scientific thinking has cut us off from that understanding of humanity through which we can recognize living human beings and the totality of their existence, not simply in the formal way of today, but in recognition of the true inner essence of human existence, namely, human development. This tremendously antihuman attitude of modern pedagogy has a symptom I have often mentioned here. When we say such things today, people may accuse us of a paradox; however, we must say them because of their importance. The loss of a truly living understanding of humanity has led to a hopeless and desolate area of experimental psychology (I have nothing against experimental psychology, per se), namely, intelligence tests—a horror story of contemporary education. I have often said that psychologists experimentally test human memory and even intellect to determine, by "objective" means, whether someone has a good or bad memory, or is intelligent or not. In this purely mechanical procedure, psychologists give sentences that the person being tested must complete, or other such things. In this way, they attempt to create a picture of the capabilities of developing human beings. This is a symptom of how our society has lost everything productive in the direct relationships between people. Intelligence testing is a symptom of the rising modern desolation that people see as especially progressive and arises from psychological research in modern universities. People can never comprehend what it means to create a pedagogy full of life and able to achieve truly free minds, unless they understand that we must return to an intuitive understanding of human nature received directly from the human being, from the developing human being. They can never comprehend this living education unless they are able to overcome the cleft that exists between one person and another. To make something of pedagogy, we must sweep all this experimenting on people out of our schools. Experimental psychology can be a valuable basis of psychology, but when it sneaks into pedagogy and even into the courtrooms, it ruins everything that requires healthy development, that needs fully developed people not separated by a gulf from other fully developed people. We have brought things so far that we have excluded everything human from our society's goals. We must change this to again include the human element. We must have the courage to energetically put a stop to much of the "progress" that has slowly built up in recent times, otherwise we will never get any further. So often today those students who leave the colleges to become teachers, leave filled with the most upside-down views about human beings. They do not receive real views because such superficial ideas as experimental tests of intelligence have replaced those views. We must recognize this as a symptom of decay. We must seek in ourselves the ability to determine another's capacities because others are human beings as we ourselves are. We must see that all other methods are ill-fated because they are devoid of the direct living comprehension of the human element so necessary if we are to move forward in a healthy way.

Modern people do not see these things at all, but they are very important if we are to move forward. How often we have spoken of these things. You have often smiled about some of these idiocies, but you have not always understood the reason for speaking of them and why they have become a part of our modern thinking. Today, it is not important that you hear these things the way you would read a feature article in the newspaper. That you learn to differentiate between witty remarks or observations and thoughts that contain a seed for action is important. All anthroposophic activity culminates in creating an idea of human beings and providing an understanding of human beings. We need that. We need it because our times demand that we overcome a threefold predicament. Three tyrannies remain from the past. First, the oldest tyranny, masked in various ways at present, is the priestly tyranny. We would progress further in our consideration of the present situation if we could recognize that this masquerade no longer exists in conjunction with facts, but unfortunately still exists in human thinking about government and about the impulses arising in Europe, America, and Asia. This is the modern disguise of the ancient priestly tyranny.

The second oppression arose somewhat later in human historical development, namely, political tyrannies, which now occur in various forms.

The third thing came relatively recently, and that is economic tyranny.

Humanity must work itself out of these three tyrannical inclinations. That is its immediate task. This will be possible only when we see where the residues of these different masks live in us today, these three tyrannies existing in humanity.

Today, it is important to raise educators' views to the level where we can discuss such things, and where we can bring the light we receive from such understanding to current events. Educators' views must be at the level where we can see how this or that compulsion everywhere hides behind various facts of the present time. However, we must now have the courage to say that because pedagogy has distanced itself from the real world, in a sense has withdrawn into the schools, it has come to the point of generating such twisted ideas. The experimental testing of human capabilities is only one symptom of this. We can see the result of the state forcing pedagogy to withdraw into the schools and to distance itself from life wherever modern people speak of general or special education methods. At present (I am expressly saying "at present" and, particularly, in our region of the world), we cannot fully develop the principal realms of life, namely, the cultural, the rights or political, and the economic realms, unless we set them upon their own feet. It is somewhat different for us than for the extreme West, that is, America, and the extreme East, but just because it is different for us, it is so important that we realize this fact. We must ultimately come to think concretely and not abstractly, otherwise we will arrive at a theory that delights humanity throughout the world and is nonsense, or, in historical development, at a kind of thousand-year Reich that is just as much nonsense. Thinking concretely in this area means to think for a specific part of the world and a specific time. We will have more to say about that later today.

Educators must direct their attention toward these major world events. They must see what exists in modern cultural life and what they must change to educate children much differently than the way they themselves were drilled. What we have recently cultivated has led to a horrible specialization in the field of education and in teachers. In lectures and at scientific or academic gatherings, we often hear songs of praise for specialization. If I could not see the reasons for academic specialization, I would, of course, be irresponsible. However, we need to balance this specialization because otherwise we will build walls between people, and we would no longer meet other human beings with understanding. We would face one another helplessly as one specialist confronting another and would have nothing upon which to base our trust in a specialist other than the fact that he or she has been officially certified in some way or another. Through the schools we are now on the path of bringing this specialization into daily life. It remains to be seen whether the present-day confusion will protect us from the affliction, suggested by many, of having psychologists, along with all the other courtroom specialists, perform their experiments on the accused as they do now on young people. I am not so very opposed to these things in themselves, but I oppose the way they have slipped into modern life.

This is how things are in pedagogy, in the schools, and in government.

After the short time when people spoke of inherent human rights, or, as they called them, natural rights (it does not matter whether these were contestable or not), the age came when people were embarrassed to discuss these natural rights. People called anyone who spoke of natural rights, a dilettante. They called anyone who thought rights were connected with the existence of human beings as individuals, a dilettante. "Professionally," people could speak only of historical rights, that is, what had historically developed as a right. People lacked the courage to recognize true rights, and therefore limited themselves to a discussion of "historical rights." Educators today must be particularly aware of this. In their professional conferences, educators must learn of the nineteenth century developments and how we lost the concept of natural rights, or, at best, allowed it to live on only in a disguised form. They must understand people's persistent wavering and inner doubt in the face of what is merely historical. If you understand the situation, you know that the prevailing trend still moves toward historical rights, only we no longer notice its extreme forms when it sneaks into pedagogy. To use Goethe's words, people take pains not to speak of inherent rights; they avoid speaking of such rights at all costs. In my lectures here, I have often noted that now we must openly and honestly enter the day of reckoning and put it off no longer. For this reason, we can no longer shy away from clearly stating what we need to eliminate, since we can never rebuild human habits of thinking and feeling unless we have a clear idea of what ruined them.

In our Middle European society, we can easily see how a genuinely positive idea of government collapsed. At the beginning of the nineteenth century, people's attempts to create a positive government failed because historical forces replaced it with an impulse of their own. Those active in these efforts believed they worked within the boundaries of unprejudiced research, but the result was one that served only the ends of the state or the economy. The state influenced not only the administration of research, but also the content of research, particularly applied research. We have virtually no national economic policy today because free and independent thinking could not develop. Therefore, people today understand nothing when we speak of true economic laws. We see this especially in the chaotic educational system—education done in a grand style, remote from real life and withdrawn into the schoolroom. If we point out only what we should experience and not how we should experience it, a living consideration of something can never occur. The only thing we have developed in recent times is the worship of superficial experience, and that leads only to confusion, particularly when we carry it out with exactitude. We need to learn to cultivate the inner disposition that leads us toward a proper view of experience.

You may recall that last Friday[2] I drew your attention, though only briefly due to the limitations of these lectures, to the way we can gain insight into the form needed for economic cooperatives by studying late-fourteenth- and early-fifteenth-century European economics. We must create the social cooperation of the future from today's urge for production and consumption. If we ground our thorough consideration of the facts in Anthroposophy, then we arrive at the basic viewpoint that the foundation of all European life lies in the events of the dawn of modern times, at the end of the fourteenth and the beginning of the fifteenth centuries. In this way, we do not falsify facts, but they guide us to those points of development whose important symptoms reveal what normally remains hidden beneath the surface and is now seen to be their driving principle. Without that insight, the inherent characteristics of the scientific method remain hidden from modern pedagogy and objective thinking. Pedagogy and research depended more or less upon chance to draw their attention to this or that area. We need inner guidelines that direct us to the important truths. We can gain these guidelines from Goethe's world view, and they allow us to recognize a great deal. We cannot fabricate them or simply seek them in the intellect. We must seek them in the picture of how human beings are interwoven with the world, and in how we have totally lost sight of this. We can see how much we have lost sight of this fact in that we so superficially want to fathom individual human beings through that pedagogical diversion, experimental psychology.

Above all, children's teachers must gain insight about the core of modern development. If we now stand at a point where we must change the main direction of life, it is most important that we comprehend what has previously occurred in human development. First to go under was a basic impulse toward a governmental life free of economics. Then, beginning in the last third of the nineteenth century, particularly in Middle Europe, we trod upon our cultural life and, frankly, made it into a parasite. How much has entered our modern cultural life of the great impulses of Goetheanism, for example? Nothing, virtually nothing! People speak superficially about Goethe, but nothing of the tremendous things in Goethe's way of seeing the world has entered general consciousness. I have often mentioned that the leadership of the Goethe Society in Weimar found it impossible to think of putting someone at the head of the society who understood something of Goethe. They could accept only a washed-up

Prussian finance minister. I also mentioned that we could easily smile at this choice, since his first name is Double Cross Yourself [Kreuzwendedich].

In this way, we have sailed into a position of discounting our cultural heritage. Nowhere in our modern consciousness can we find an imprint of Goethe's viewpoint upon German cultural life. We have eliminated all of that, thus turning cultural life into a parasite. Edition after edition of Goethe has been published, but nowhere has Goethe's spirit been absorbed. If you can see through such things, you must admit that today things are terrible in the realm of economics, things are terrible in the realm of politics, but in the cultural realm, things are the worst. First, we ruined our political consciousness, then our connection to our own cultural life. I do not say this to be pessimistic, but because what we must do must arise out of an insight into what has occurred.

Then came what people call the World War. After the collapse of political life, which people continued to prop up, and the inner collapse of cultural life, came the economic collapse. People today have no idea of the magnitude of this because they believe we are at the end, or possibly the middle, of this collapse. We are actually only at the beginning. You can study this economic collapse; everywhere you see what has become a world catastrophe. If you objectively study what occurred with the so-called Baghdad Railway affair[3] before the war, then you will see the most unfortunate interconnections between political and economic life. If you follow the individual stages of the Baghdad Railway negotiations, particularly those connected with the unfortunate Mr. Helfferich[4] then you can see, on the one hand, the formation of one capitalistic cartel after another, and, on the other, the influence of national political chauvinistic intrigues. These intrigues were different depending upon whether they arose in the East or in the West. In Germany, we see the loss of conscious activity because we had lost cultural life and political life; we limited everything to economic life. From the West, economic and political aspirations played in everywhere, carrying the disguise of chauvinism or nationalism or economic policy. From the East, cultural policies played in, disguised in various manners. All of this came together in a ball of confusion that then resulted in the absurdity of the Baghdad affair. The Baghdad Railway affair and the entire sequence of events provide proof of the impossibility of further developing the old imperialism, that is, the impossibility of further developing the old political system.

What we could see in a major world political problem, namely, in the will to construct this railway, we could also see in individual instances during the war. People have simply never considered things so that factual guidelines could bring them to the point where external events reveal their inner connections. Here you have it: Kapp[5] shrieked, Bethmann Hollweg[6] whined, and the cultural representatives of Germany were silent. This was the situation. Kapp, the representative of agriculture, shrieked because he didn't know which way to turn between the problems of the war economy and the problems of agriculture. Bethmann Hollweg, who had no head for politics, whined because he didn't know how to say anything reasonable about the situation. The cultural leaders of Germany remained silent because they had completely withdrawn into academic ivory towers and knew nothing of life or how to handle things in life.

I do not know how many of you remember this affair. I haven't exaggerated anything at all; it really was the situation that Kapp shrieked and Bethmann Hollweg whined in the Reichstag about the terrible way he, the poor man, had been treated. Those who should have known something about such things were quiet or only spoke about things distant from life.

Only a conspicuous absurdity could have demonstrated the nature of economic progress. Many people never have noticed how we have slid regarding the government. They had their Hohenzollerns, their Habsburgs, their Romanov Czars. People could delude themselves about the fact that the seed of destruction lay within Czarism, or the Hohenzollern dynasty, or the Habsburg dynasty because the artificial framework held together what was already moving toward dissolution because governmental ideals no longer existed.

Modern socialists often emphasize that the state must cease to exist, but no one has done more to cause the cessation of reasonable government than the European dynasties of the nineteenth century. Through illusions and self-deception we could deceive ourselves about the fact that we beat cultural life into the ground during the nineteenth century, but concerning economic life, that is not possible. When the state is starving, it consoles itself with festivities and brings paper flowers to dynasties. It is no fairy tale, but in fact, provable, that, to have them as souvenirs, well-dressed women fell upon the cigarette butts Wilhelm II threw away on the Hamburg bridges. It is also not a fairy tale that the selfsame Wilhelm II did not turn away in disgust from such goings-on, but, in his pomposity, saw them as positive. He was, in fact, delighted by them.

In the economic area, we have experienced such unusual events that we cannot characterize them other than to say that agriculture squealed, politics whined, and industry rubbed its stomach because it felt so good. At first the workers, at least while they still received some crumbs from industry, also rubbed their stomachs, until they went to the front and learned a different tune. Then they spread other viewpoints when they returned home. Anyone who claims that the collapse began at home is clearly lying. The collapse actually began at the front lines because people could no longer bear the situation.

Today, teachers in particular must know such things. They can no longer sit in a quiet corner and know nothing of life. Instead, they must know what we must do. Today, instead of discussing formalities at their conferences, it is more important that the teachers of our youth speak openly about these historical events and bring to light what we can so clearly show in the area of capitalist economics.

You are certainly aware that one side claims and the other denies a sentence attributed to a particular society, namely, "The end justifies the means." Under the influence of capitalism, a quite different impulse has become apparent in economic life during this world catastrophe, namely, the end condemns the means. Everywhere you look—you can see this specifically with the Baghdad Railway problem—the means invalidate the goals, or, on the other hand, the goals invalidate the means.

We must be aware of such things, and we must pursue them relentlessly. Insofar as I have directed my remarks today toward pedagogy, I believe that we must speak to teachers at every level in this way. (Perhaps, not in the way I am speaking, but at least from this direction.) We must outgrow what has, until now, kept teachers at various levels from being told of great world events, causing our present experience of the absolute political naiveté of a large segment of the population. Now you meet people who have not the faintest idea of what the proletarian movement has been doing for decades, not even its most superficial activities. I cannot be polite about this, since I cannot even say, "Present company excluded," at least not all. Such people do not have the slightest idea how the proletariat has struggled for decades. An education that sends people out into the world so that they simply pass one another by and know nothing of one another inevitably leads to a collapse. Are there not middle-class people today who know virtually nothing more about the workers than that they dress differently, who know nothing of the striving that lives in the unions and political parties, and who make no effort whatsoever to really look at what is going on around them? Why is this? Because people never learned how to learn from life; they only learned how to know this or that. People think to themselves, "I know this, I am a specialist in this area; you know that, you are a specialist in that area." People have accustomed themselves to this kind of thinking. They have never gone further than the knowledge absorbed in school and consider the absorption of such knowledge as the ideal. However, what is truly important is that people learn to learn, that they learn to learn so they can remain a student of life even when they become old, right until death. Today, people, even if they have graduated from a college, generally stop learning after they reach their twenties. They can no longer learn from life. They only drone on and on about what they have learned until then; at best they occasionally add something. Those who are different are the exception today. It is important that we find a way to teach how to learn, that is, how to learn throughout life from life. We can always learn something from life. We would be in a quite different situation today if people had learned to learn. Why are we so socially helpless today? Because people are not equal to the events of today. They cannot learn from events because they always cling to appearances. In the future, education will not bear fruit if we do not make the effort to raise ourselves to the higher viewpoints of human society.

Anyone who looks at today's world with just a little anthroposophic background will know how to think concretely about current events. People can look to the West and to the East and derive tasks from specific observations. Looking to the West, into the Anglo-American world, we see the great political impulses that have been so detrimental to us here in Middle

Europe, but have played such a large role in the last decades, perhaps longer. All those major impulses that have entered modern political life began with the Anglo-American peoples, because they have always known how to take historical forces into account. During the war, when I tried to tell people that we could counter the forces that arise in the West only with similar forces derived from historical impulses, they laughed at me, because they did not believe in the great historical impulses.

If you study the Anglo-American West, you will find there a number of human instincts and tendencies arising from historical life. All these inclinations have a political-economic nature. There are important basic tendencies within the Anglo-American culture, all of which have a political-economic color so that those peoples think of economics politically. However, there is something peculiar about this. You know that when we speak about economics, we **demand** that fraternity rule economy in the future. However, just this fraternity was forced out of the Western imperialistic political-economic movement. Fraternity was left out, it was shut out, and for this reason, what is alive there has a strongly capitalistic character.

Fraternity developed in the East. If you study the East in connection with its entire spiritual and soul aspects, then you will see that a sense of fraternity pours out of people there. What was so unusual in the West was the flood of economic life under an antisocial influence, an economic life that thus tends toward capitalism. In the East, we find fraternity without economics. We in Middle Europe held these two tendencies apart. One of the important things teachers must know is that we have the task of creating a synthesis of the East's sense of fraternity with the West's antisocial economic thinking. If we can do this, we will achieve socialization in the larger sense.

Let us now look at the East from the proper perspective. We find there even in ancient times a highly developed spiritual life, and only someone who does not understand Rabindranath Tagore[7] could claim that it is now dead. There, people live a spiritual-political life. That is in the East. Where is its opposite? That is, again, in the West. Something is missing from the spiritual-political life of the East, namely, freedom. In the East, a kind of subjugation exists which leads to the renunciation of the human Self in Brahma or Nirvana. This is the contradiction of all freedom. The West, on the other hand, has mastered freedom. We stand in the middle and must form a synthesis. We can do this if we clearly separate freedom and fraternity in life and have the balance to do so. We must not understand our task as imagining that what is good for one is good for everyone, since thinking so abstractly would be the ruin of all genuine desire. People destroy all thinking consistent with reality when they believe they can set up some worldwide unified abstract ideal or wish to determine a modern social organization valid for all time. This is not only nonsense, but also a sin against reality because every area and every time has its own tasks, and we must recognize them. We cannot be so lazy as not to look at the realities of specific human relationships, and we must recognize as our task that we learn to study facts in their proper perspective. Modern public education has brought us even further away from a proper interpretation of events. It has no desire to know anything about concrete specific events, since modern people begin to feel so uncertain just here. Today people want to define rather than characterize. They want to accept only superficial events rather than to see events as symptoms of the underlying impulses.

I am speaking today such that all I have to say can be drawn from the way we must now speak about pedagogy. Today, the best teachers are those who can properly understand what comes from this direction and not those who can tell us only what they know about this or that subject. Anyone can gain knowledge of a particular subject by reading a handbook or encyclopedia while preparing for a class. In the future, teaching examinations must answer the question of how people are as people. When applied to pedagogy, this kind of cultural life requires that we do not prepare people in an unbalanced manner for their work, but that we prepare them to actually apply spiritual activity to all three aspects of human nature. I certainly do not suggest that those who have never lifted a hammer can never see truth properly and can never stand in cultural life properly. We can achieve this by having people move about in the three areas of the social organism, having them make real connections with all three areas, and working, truly working, in all three. Possibilities to do this will arise, but we must hammer a sense of it into the heads of those who would teach our youth in the future.

A sense for something else will also awaken, namely, a sense of something that goes beyond specialization, something we are attempting to create through Anthroposophy. We must see to it that the thread connecting us to a general consideration of what is human and to the insight into what the human being actually is, never breaks. We must keep people from drowning in specialization even though they must be good specialists. This demands a much more active life than modern people are often comfortable with.

At various academic and technical conferences I have often had an extremely unfortunate experience. People come together in these conferences with the express intention of furthering their subject, and they often do this for hours, quite diligently and zealously. However, I have frequently heard an unusual expression, namely, "shop talk." People wanted only to find some time where they no longer "talked shop," that is, no longer talked about their specialty. Sometimes, they spoke of the dumbest things, the most boring things, but they no longer talked shop. People talked about all kinds of things, sometimes good things, but they frowned upon that. In short, people were happy when they no longer had to talk shop. That people are happy to get away from what they do, and should do, for humanity just illustrates how little connection they have with their work. Now I ask you, if leaders who so quickly attempt to run away from their specialties can ever understand a population so desirous of and willing to work? If you smugly talk about everything that is wrong with the working classes today, then you have not asked the working classes what created these wrongs, but instead have asked the middle-class people who created the problems and are everywhere. Those harnessed to a dying capitalism as workers cannot find a place in society where they can find happiness in their work, if those who stand above them always slip quickly out of work they should happily undertake. These are the ethical side-effects of our modern pedagogy. This is what is most important to see and most important to change. A great deal exists in the thinking habits of teachers that must become quite different in the future.

What did I want to discuss in this lecture? I wanted to make clear to you how radically we must present what must occur today. I wanted to present the absolute necessity that we rise above the trivia, the terrible details, into which we have forced the content of our thought and our entire life of feeling and willing. How is will to blossom—we need this will for the future—if it remains trapped in the habit of small caliber thinking and feeling?

What do we need for the future that we do not have today? We need a genuine human psychology. We need to know everything about developing human beings, but we have shut out this knowledge. Instead, we have examination methods that experiment around on people, unable to enter intuitively into human individuality. These methods purport to reveal people's capabilities, but we no longer trust ourselves to point out the discrepancies. Why? Because we lack sufficient interest in such things. Because we go through life with our souls asleep. Our souls must awaken. We must really look at things. Then we will see the absurdity of much that we honor as tremendous progress today. These poor elementary school teachers, whom we send out like tame rabbits, cannot see anything of what actually lives in the world. They raise children in the same way they pass by their fellow human beings, without the slightest idea of what lives in their souls. Quite independent of the fact that many in the middle class have no will at all to address the dominant current problems and impulses, those who do have will are barely useful, since they have no idea what is necessary. They have completely slept through the decades when, day after day, the proletariat schooled itself politically. Today, we seldom hear workers complaining about having too little time or being too busy when the need arises to speak about major problems in our time. They make the time. If you approach middle-class groups, they never have time to look into current problems—they all have so much to do. But this is not the real reason. They actually do not have the slightest idea how to consider such problems. They are totally unable to really tackle a problem, since no one ever taught them to do this.

This is not simply a pessimistic viewpoint nor is it meant as a tirade. I am simply stating the facts. We have experienced that where life has forced people to learn, they have learned; but where their own motivation could have led people to learn, nothing happened, nothing at all. This is why we stand in the middle of such misery today, and why we hear in everything attempted today, not only in expressions of ill will (there is certainly enough of that) but in all the other nonsense that comes simply from a lack of knowledge of life: No schools took the trouble to teach how to learn from life. Some knowledge did trickle through the walls of comfort and reached people, but this did not happen because people were taught to confront the events of life with wide-awake senses.

Those who continue to talk in the old way, who seem to have wound the clockworks of their brains and are now letting them tick, could learn much from the sad events of the present. They hold conferences today in just the same manner as before the catastrophe of this war. Great numbers of people have learned little from these terrible events, because they have simply not grasped how to learn. Now, due to the suffering, they must learn what they did not learn from the frightening events of the past. Some time ago I mentioned Herman Grimm,[8] a quite wise and well-educated observer of life, whom I also mentioned in my book *Towards Social Renewal*. Back in the 1890s, this man said, "If you look around at life and the direction in which it is rushing, namely, in the direction of unrestrained armament, then you have to admit that you would like to fix a day of general suicide. Life has become so hopeless." People wanted to live in dreams and illusions, and those who called themselves practical wanted this the most. However, today we must wake up. Those who do not wake up cannot work upon what we need so much today, what each individual human being needs so much. Many people do not even know which end of the hammer to grab.

I wanted to say this, in a sense, as the kind of discussion we should hold at today's teachers' conferences. We should develop these thoughts with the people who are to teach our youth, since they need to see what must occur. When we continue these observations, we will go further into things specific to pedagogy and education.

THE SOCIAL BASIS OF
PUBLIC EDUCATION

3

STUTTGART, JUNE 1, 1919

TODAY, IT IS EXTREMELY IMPORTANT that we see the deeper connections existing within human society. It is a symptom of our times that people are often satisfied with superficial opinions, that is, opinions gained through simply observing the surface of life. This has led to a situation in which one person considers something true and another person considers it false, but neither knows what to do with these opinions of true and false. People do not know what to do with these views because, although they can form thoughts about things that lie on the surface, they never achieve anything practical when they try to put these thoughts into effect. Reality does not accept superficial beliefs as easily as people do in their heads. That easy acceptance is one of the cancers of modern times. Another cancer is that people do not want to exercise the introspection that, at the right moment, might tell them that such ideas arise out of a self-interest they cannot manipulate into a social goal. We may not say that something we do in our personal interest is also a social deed. We see much of this sort of thing, much more often than in years past. We repeatedly find that our desires have become the self-serving deeds of a particular group, and then people say that the results are consequences of what we wanted. Here I am only pointing out that today we must have the goodwill to look into things more deeply and to get past simple superficial points of view.

Nowhere is the need to overcome superficial opinions more necessary, and nowhere is the goodwill to do this more lacking, than in the area of education. If we in education are really to think socially, then we must turn our attention to even the most basic details. You have perhaps seen this in the two previous lectures on pedagogy, but I hope you will keep this particularly in mind as you listen now.

Just look at people's experience, beginning as the youngest children in the lowest grades. When young children enter school, practically everything except the needs and desires of the developing human being determines what happens. As they progress from grade to grade, this becomes worse and worse. At an age when children can least tolerate it, something like the following occurs. A child goes to the first class of the morning. For the convenience of the faculty, the child has, for instance, mathematics or arithmetic in the first period; then, perhaps Latin, then, maybe a period of religion. After that, there is music or singing, but maybe not even that, and, instead, geography. We cannot more fundamentally ruin human nature than by teaching children in this manner. This absolutely destroys the child's powers of concentration. The class schedule, this nemesis of all genuine education, must be our starting point in socializing education. Today, we must fight most strongly against class schedules throughout all the grades.

Even when we only think of bringing health to the educational system we must take care that the child remains with a subject as long as necessary at his or her developmental stage. Suppose, for example, that we discover at what age we should teach mathematical or physical concepts to a developing human being. Then, we must not choose the worst path, setting aside one or three or five hours a week for this subject; rather, we must devote a block to this. That means we must allow the child to concentrate upon a subject for a certain period without being continually disturbed by other things. We must use a pedagogically and psychologically oriented anthropology to become clear about the stage of life in which we should, for example, teach children arithmetic. Then, when we focus upon arithmetic, we must focus upon it throughout the day. Of course, I do not mean that the child should do only arithmetic from morning until night. I mean it in the way that I once had to teach an eleven-year-old child with serious soul disturbances.[1] In that case, I attempted to proceed efficiently. Out of all the people responsible for educating this child, I reserved the right to develop the entire teaching plan when I wanted to focus attention on a particular thing. That is, I reserved the right to determine how much time the boy would spend playing the piano, how much time he would sing, and so forth. It was not my intent simply to fill his soul with a particular amount of learning material, but to direct his entire development so that his soul could concentrate upon something during a particular period of life. I intended that his soul reach a definite conclusion in a specific area of human development before turning to something else. To put it another way, we need to think about how much arithmetic we need to teach a child at a particular age, and then close this period so that the developing child has the feeling of having achieved something. Only then can we continue on to another topic.

You can see from this that all the way through school the basis of modern teaching contains something fundamentally destructive. There can hardly be anything more contradictory than when a student enters school and, as I did in my time, hears something like this:

First Period: Practical Philosophy
Second Period: History
Third Period: Literature
Fourth Period: Civics
and so forth.

The intent here was not what it should have been, namely, to avoid confusing the developing child. The intent here was simply to satisfy the organizational convenience of the school. We can say this completely without prejudice.

Today, we have one primary task before us. Given the pervasiveness of current thinking habits, it is hard to believe that society in general has an inclination to grapple with this task. This is what I mean when I say that today is the time of the great day of reckoning. People often believe we can be equal to the great day of reckoning if we just speak in large words. We can meet it, though, only if we approach great changes with inner courage and do not lose that courage when we meet opposition to these great changes.

Today, the public holds something else as nearly indispensable, and that has great importance, particularly for the lower grades, namely, the State Board of Accreditation. Nothing can be more detrimental for a proper development of cultural life than such official or semi-official review boards. What the school system really needs, and anyone who can look into the deeper aspects of things knows this, what it needs for genuinely fruitful development is continuous observation of the results of the living nature of teaching. No board standing outside the school can ever judge this, nor should it. You may not meddle in the methods or such of someone to whom, with due precaution, you have given cultural self-determination and have entrusted the teaching and education of other people. This is something many people do not understand today, but with this lack of understanding they also do not understand one of the basic conditions of a maturing cultural life. From this, you can see the radical way we must change everything modern people accept as a matter of course and even demand be increased. It is difficult to find anywhere a social program arising out of political party thinking that does not include some kind of official or semi-official accreditation of schools. Here I am not accusing anyone, including any of the parties, of anything; I am simply pointing out an absurdity that has occurred gradually in cultural life.

We can easily study these cultural absurdities by looking at higher education. How have we actually developed higher education? We could still see that development in the second half of the nineteenth century. In the end, everyone who achieved something of world importance in German cultural life, grew up during a time when the modern system had not yet destroyed the basis of a true spiritual development. Goethe certainly complained about all the hurdles placed in his way during his education. It would definitely be worthwhile to consider how what he writes about Professor Ludwig and other people in *Dichtung und Wahrheit* [Poetry and Truth] would appear had Goethe been forced into a restrictive modern college at the age of eighteen or nineteen. We need to look at such things today.

What, actually, have we slowly destroyed? When the college preparatory high schools, which are such a nightmare in relation to modern demands, were the only way to prepare for entry into the university, they still had the characteristics of the old cloister high schools, which were really not so bad for their time. They still retained some characteristics that enabled students to absorb things that raised them to the level of a general view of the world. These schools still included basic courses in the curriculum, although only in the last two years. Of course, they usually taught what students should study in the second year in the first, and what belonged in the first year, in the second. At least they studied it, though. A little remained of the old colleges, namely, that in the first years, students had an opportunity to receive a general education that then enabled them to direct their studies toward a particular profession. Obviously, no one can achieve anything in a particular profession who has not gained an understanding of general human life through some form of preparatory instruction. Today, people consider it superfluous to teach students logical or psychological concepts. No one can advantageously study any area of cultural life without having previously obtained some idea of logic and psychology and, in a certain sense, without having gained the right to such study. Modern cultural life has completely destroyed these things. We no longer want to look at the human being, but instead want to train people according to motives quite foreign to cultural life.

This has led to a situation in which our general intellectual and artistic activities no longer carry the imprint of a unified culture. Our cultural life has divided us so that we can no longer accomplish what we must accomplish. Those with experience in this area know how often modern people praise specialization. They emphasize that science and the arts have become so broad that people can be fruitful only when they master a particular specialty. This is, of course, obvious when seen from one side; however, an inner need for comfort has prompted people to embrace this most obvious thing with remarkable lust. Now you need do nothing more than encapsulate yourself in some specialty and, simply because you have encapsulated yourself in a specialty, people will look upon you as a particularly distinguished person. Of course, no one who really values culture would want specialization to revert to an all-pervasive amateurism. We must work to so structure the entire system of education that people will understand semiconsciously that they can connect their specialties with the entirety of culture. That can happen only when higher education rests upon a foundation of general education. But then pedants will object by asking, "What about professional training?" We need only see how efficiently we can proceed when students have a general education and understand what is truly human before they begin training in specialties and professions. Today, we are so deeply imbedded in our perverse situation that we can be extremely well developed in our specialty and total idiots about all the great questions of humanity. Today, we have the curious situation that those who enjoyed only an elementary school education, and perhaps not even that, but were dragged through life, have more and better things to say about the general human condition than those who received higher education and are quite excellent in their specific fields.

Today, we must fight against this situation if we want to send impulses deep into it, impulses that alone can lead to an improvement. If we want something to occur, we must not simply act superficially, as many people want, that is, we must not act in a way counter to the demands of reality. Today, the problem is that we have carried this error so far that it is hardly possible to find the people needed for such a foundation of the colleges. We are in the terrible position that we can no longer find teachers for general education. The leading edge of our culture, the colleges, has fallen asleep. We experience it today when, in our colleges, a professor just reads lectures about some science from published class notes, so that students can simply buy them to drill themselves in preparation for an exam. This is even a rather common occurrence, but what does it really mean? It means that the students completely wasted the time used to listen to the lecture, because what really occurred was only that the professor drilled the class notes into them. When a student reads the class notes, then everything that really needs to happen has occurred. It is completely unnecessary and superfluous for a professor to stand up at the podium and read the class notes aloud.

Someone could easily say that I stand here before you, a philistine demanding the abolition of the faculty! I certainly do not demand the abolition of college faculties, I only want to point out that professors give lectures today with total disregard of the fact that we now know how to print books. Things simply read aloud really can penetrate the old noggin if read in properly written books. However, I would also like to make you aware that you can, at best, get from a well-written book a tenth of what you can get directly from a teacher whose teaching creates a connection between the souls of the teacher and the student. This can only happen, though, in a free and independent cultural life where individuals can develop completely. It cannot happen where tradition such as we find in universities and colleges still has the same upper hand it has had for centuries, but only where individuals can be themselves right down to the smallest details. Then, we could say about the practice of oral teaching that we have broken with everything that comes to humanity through publishing and illustrations and so forth. Because we would have thrown that out, we would then have the possibility of developing completely new capacities in teaching, which now only sleep in humanity. Such things are part and parcel of the current social questions. Only when we have the heart and mind for such things can we work toward what is so necessary today.

Let us now look at the general social situation that results from the perversion of higher education. In my public lecture yesterday,[2] I remarked that we find essentially no reflection of the true social situation in the economic policies of either the bourgeoisie or the proletariat, simply because we did not have the strength to develop a true social science. What has arisen under the bourgeoisie in place of social science? Something that people are quite proud of, that they never become tired of praising again and again, namely, modern sociology. Modern sociology is the most nonsensical area of study possible, since it sins against all the most elementary requirements of a social science. Sociology seeks to show its prowess by avoiding everything that could lead to social will and social motivation. It simply records historical and statistical "sociological facts" in an attempt to prove that human beings are a kind of social animal living in a society. Sociology provides this proof, strongly though unconsciously, by bringing nothing more to the light of day than sociological platitudes, things trivial and generally known. Nowhere does a desire to discover the laws of society and their connection to human social willing exist. This is how this specialty completely incapacitates the human spirit. We must openly admit that the modern non-proletarian classes absolutely lack social will. Social will is completely missing because sociology replaced social science in the colleges that should have nurtured social will. An impotent sociology has replaced a social science that could have stimulated people and pulsed throughout their wills.

Such things are deeply rooted in cultural life, and we must seek them there if we are ever to understand them. We need only think about how different people's lives would be if what I spoke of in a previous lecture came to pass. If, at the subtle birth of their sentient souls, around the age of fourteen or fifteen, we directed students' attention not toward ancient civilizations formed under quite different social conditions, but instead introduced things close at hand in modern life, the students could learn directly what happens in those fields, in the trades and in commerce. People should learn all this. Imagine how differently they would then move on into life. Imagine how self-reliant they would be. Imagine how they would refuse to have forced upon them what people praise so often today as the epitome of culture, but what is in actuality nothing other than the worst form of decadence.

Art, for example, can flourish only on the soil of a self-determined cultural life. Genuine art arises from the people. Art is, in its most noble sense, social. Someone who studies Greek or Roman or Gothic architecture in the way often done today knows very little. You can know what lies in Greek, Roman, or Gothic architecture only if you understand the social structure of the periods when these styles were current and can see in their styles and forms, lines and impressions, how art swayed the human soul. What people did every day, right into their finger movements, was a continuation of what they saw when they looked at the things that gave them an opportunity to experience genuine reality, say, when they looked at an architectural style. Today, we must marry art with life, but this marriage can flourish only on the soil of a free cultural life. What a pity that we take our children into schoolrooms where they meet with the most barbaric surroundings for their young souls! You need only imagine how it would be for children to learn their times tables in classrooms that were not decorated in the "artistic" way of today, but were decorated by an artist so that everything the eye fell upon was in harmony.

Socially effective thoughts cannot exist unless a supporting spiritual impulse radiates into the soul during the time these thoughts form, an impulse that comes from a truly living environment. For example, artists need a much different course of life than they now enjoy while growing up. Today, those with an inner artistic desire have absolutely no possibility of experiencing life. If someone feels, for instance, a desire to become a painter, then life forces that person to dash off some kitsch as soon as possible because it is believed to be important to create something that gives inner satisfaction. Of course, that is important, but what is really important is that the impulse for this inner satisfaction first find a path into life, so that the artist can feel the greatest possible satisfaction when he or she asks life what to create. You feel the greatest possible inner satisfaction when you feel a responsibility to take nothing from life that you cannot give back. Art is not served today when, for instance, a painter provides landscape paintings for people who understand little of them. On the contrary, art is thrown into the gutter. Thus, we have unnecessary consumer art along with a barbarically formed living environment. Suppose the condition that my book on the social question[3] attempted to bring about were to come about, so that any means of production would enter the social structure unencumbered for the simple reason that it can cost something only until its construction is complete.[4] Imagine then, how all individual egotistical interests would disappear, and how the desire to create for all of humanity would arise instinctively and intuitively. Imagine how people would search for ways to create for all of humanity instead of ways to create for capitalists and their non-needs.[5] Our primary task is to socialize in such a way that all cultural life does not fall under the wheels of state socialism.

On this matter our leaders have not the slightest inclination to look at what is right. Our leaders see the Spartacists and the Bolsheviks[6] as scandalous, but neither group made themselves what they are. Who made them what they are? Our leaders! Our leaders have felt no desire to found a genuine popular culture. If our leaders had fulfilled their responsibilities, there would be no Bolsheviks and no Spartacists. Apart from that, the Spartacists and the Bolsheviks are just not the way our leaders paint them. Our leaders color them the way they do in order to present the world with a horror show that justifies their armies. But this is only a digression.

Today, our leaders need to honestly look at themselves in the mirror, but they have little inclination to do so.

You see, human development has not yet torn out of the soul what we need to improve it. It is still in the soul, particularly in the German people. However, the German people have long avoided developing the seeds of their own thoughts and feelings. The lower grades in school have inoculated them with what has turned the great German people into political automatons, machines blindly following the dictates of their government. There is a direct connection between all the terrible things we see around us and this wrong education, an education that does not develop free and independent people because it itself is not free and independent. The closer its ties to the state, the more comfortable the educational system feels. Educators have concluded countless conferences on education with the resolution that they have full confidence that the present government will do what is necessary in Versailles—drum us out of the civilized world. In countless conferences, educators pass resolutions in complete support of the government. In truth, there is almost no one in the government who belongs there, and our greatest need is to admit honestly that everything occurring there is simply a continuation of the disaster that occurred in Germany during the tragic year of 1914. The errors in our educational system influence all these things. The failure of our educational system has robbed people of the ability to comprehend life's events.

As I have already mentioned, just as a reasonable school system, concerned more about concentration than about ill-conceived schedules, would develop a level of self-reliant understanding and reasoning in people, in the same way, people would properly value will if education truly permeated society with the social arts. No one can have will who has not learned how to will through a genuinely artistic education. One of the basic requirements of the future psychological pedagogy is to recognize the secret connection of art with life, and, in particular, with the human will. We must base all future pedagogy on psychology. Given that psychology has been forced out of people and has disappeared from our education, the creators of this future psychology must be artists who still have a little psychology flowing in their veins. In scientific education, not even the tiniest bit of psychology remains. People could have such a good life if each person really worked for everyone and everyone worked for each person,[7] because then we could organize production so that time would be available for such an education. People would not say much of the humbug of today if they wanted to speak honestly and if we met the needs of cultural life, namely, that people do both manual and mental work, something we must aim for in the future. Then, all over the Earth everyone—well, it could not be everyone, but at least an approximation of this ideal must occur—everyone would do their portion of manual labor and no one would need to work more than three or four hours per day. It is possible to demonstrate this through an approximation. The needs of human development do not demand we labor more than three or four hours per day. That some have to work more now results from—we can say this without emotion or passion as a completely objective fact—the countless do-nothings and coupon clippers roaming in our midst. We must face these things openly and honestly. We cannot correct the situation by only changing things here or there. We must change our education and our public schools so that we educate people in such a way that they can learn how to use their judgment in life.

Today, our educational system raises human plants that have not the least ability to judge the things going on around them. For this reason, all the news that comes from Versailles, for example, is so senseless. No one can judge the importance of one thing or another, or the motives that cause one nation to think one way or another, or what the people of one nation or another need due to their backgrounds. This is why people do not understand us when we talk about such things. If only a little of the nature of the threefold social organism would soak into human understanding, then people would see why what threatens us from the West would drown all political and cultural life in economics, and why what impinges upon us from the East out of Russia is humanity's cry for the salvation of cultural life from economics. Two extremes confront one another, the West and the East, and we in the middle have a task to be watchful of the West and avoid its errors. We must watch the East and cultivate what we must do so it is not forced upon us, in decades, not in centuries, because humanity will be forced to do what it does not do voluntarily. Here in the middle of Europe, we have the task of cultivating what we can cultivate only on a foundation of the three aspects of the social organism. If Eastern culture were to predominate today, then it would flood the Earth with nebulous mysticism, it would flood the Earth with a theosophy foreign to reality. If the West were to predominate, then it would flood and tyrannize the Earth with naked material life. Our task is to ward off these two terrible detriments to humanity through a reasoned threefolding of the social organism. In this way, economics and culture gain independence and the state no longer can take these things so far that the West and the East crush us and bring us to our demise.

An objective glance at the West shows us that now we must be attentive to everything coming from the Romantic people.

Nothing could be more dangerous for us than to lose ourselves in illusions about the deep reasons that France primarily
is working toward our demise. If we can restrain what comes
toward us from France, then we can easily overcome the
English threat. To do this, however, we need discriminating
judgment. We need to recognize that, with only a few exceptions, all those people representing Germany—I am not certain how to say this to offend no one—all the German people
negotiating the fate of Germany in Versailles are being used as
pawns. We must see the plain facts of the situation. We may
make absolutely no concessions to them in our inner judgment. If we can understand that today, then we can derive the
first impulse necessary, particularly for public education. We
can see the kind of people public education has caused to rise
to the surface, and who now determine the fate of humanity.

Of course, it is easier to make the most trivial judgments
about what I really mean than it is to begin with the suggestions I have made, to look at the various fields of human activity and to determine the right thing to do in each case. Some
time ago I spoke at our building in Dornach about the threefold social organism; time passed and a very strange plan
popped up. Perhaps I may use this plan as a grotesque example
of how we raise people today. In Dornach, we have our building, and many people work on it. Then there are other people
living in the area who have nothing to do. Now, I spoke about
the threefold social organism and afterward the obvious idea
that we must begin somewhere arose in some heads. People
wanted to begin a social experiment in some way. They proposed to do this in the most sectarian manner possible, namely,
to take a small area and cultivate the noxious weeds of selfishness. Then they could say that they had at least begun somewhere with something social. The idea was, therefore, to create
a social community among the people grouped around the

building in Dornach and to put the threefold social organism into practice. People had developed plans for putting the threefold social organism into practice in Dornach. All I could do was to ask them what they meant this to be? If you undertook this seriously, then the first thing needed would be economic independence. Of course, you would then need to buy cows and to milk them and do everything else needed to create an economic oasis. The result, however, would be the creation of economic parasites, because every such economic oasis must have a connection with people outside it and every such sectarian closure is nothing other than economic parasitism. In a closed economy, you can only live in social egotism since, when you shut things out, you then live at the expense of others. This is the worst form of capitalism. And now, the question of the rights realm: I would like to see what would happen if you were to form a court. In the event you sentence someone for some wrongdoing, I would like to see what the Swiss government would say about your threefold community! Then, we have cultural life: Since the beginning of the anthroposophic movement, we have fought against all obstacles to the creation of an independent cultural life. We have done this since the very beginning, and you do not even see that we have already begun this task. You have so little understanding for it that you think you need to create this, too.

It is of little value today when someone says we must certainly begin somewhere. What people usually mean by such a statement is the worst form of capitalistic egotism, that we must first begin by forming such a capitalistic colony. This lies extremely far from true social thinking; however, I am not intending to criticize individuals. I am the last person not to recognize the difficulties people have when they attempt to comprehend the great tasks of our times. There is something else I would warmly suggest to you, and that is, do not rock yourselves to sleep with illusions. If you want to create capitalistic egotism, admit it. Due to current conditions, you must be capitalistically egotistical for your own benefit. Admit the truth of this, because all genuine social life must begin with truth. You should not deny the truth in anything you say. You should never confront people with what is untrue, not even in the way you speak.

Today, the call for free schools goes throughout the land, but what does this really mean? A call could go throughout the land for the creation of a society in which everyone could provide the proper support for education. Education free of cost is nothing more than a lie. Hiding behind this lie is either the fact that revenue finds it way into the pockets of a small clique so they can found their school and thus gain mastery over others, or that this lie is dust thrown in people's eyes to keep them from realizing that some of their money is taken to support the schools. In the way we speak, we must always be conscientious in our striving for truth.

The task is large, but we must always keep the greatness of this task before us. Not everyone, of course, can fulfill the ideals of Anthroposophy as we have presented them for decades within a small movement. Some people need to take their professional positions into account, others, their husbands or wives, and others, the education of their children. Everyone must admit this without reservation, so that they come to realize how far they are from the real task themselves. The anthroposophic ideal requires the efforts of the entire human being. Many people cannot do that today, but they should not delude themselves that they have already done enough. Rather, they should admit the truth to themselves. On the other hand, people must fully understand that today everything stands or falls upon our efforts toward a true cultural life. Today, no one who does not dare to admit that radicalism must extend right into the details, like the change of the school class schedule, can come to a proper view of what cultural and social life need. Out of such details develop the snowballs that then grow into the avalanches of today's great cultural illnesses. Please think about this. We will speak about it again in the future.

THE TASKS OF SCHOOLS

AND THE THREEFOLD SOCIAL ORGANISM

A lecture to the Union of Young Teachers

STUTTGART, JUNE 19, 1919

I AM EXTREMELY PLEASED to be speaking to members of the teaching profession. My destiny has led me to work in various professions, and I try to understand what lives in different professions and social classes, especially within the confusion and chaos of modern times. I feel particularly at home with teachers, since I taught for many years, although in a private situation, which may not have been the ideal situation. Consequently, I also feel urged to speak specifically to that profession about reforming the human conditions that have developed.

When we look at the essence of current social demands and at clear or shadowy insights into what we must do in the future, it can be said that any reformation of our life would suffer the greatest imaginable loss if we fail to heed what teachers have to say about current needs and about what may be heard throughout the civilized world. If teachers did not direct their efforts toward improving the human condition, it would become obvious that any attempt to reform human institutions would itself require immediate improvement and could not possibly lead to any improvement.

From what I have to say, you will realize that I object to a number of things in today's educational institutions, but I ask that you don't take what I say as criticism of today's teachers. I definitely recognize that teachers suffer greatly in today's schools, that they may often ache and yet remain unaware of their pain because of life's pressures. Therefore, the deepest and most significant discussions of the so-called "social question" can take place with teachers.

Although it is seldom recognized, teachers have a tremendous personal interest in what comes of the calls for socialization, now and in the near future. We may have misgivings about the current party programs being circulated, but we are not interested in discussing them specifically. Nevertheless, those more or less radical socialist programs lead to other programs for "socializing" the school system. If we were to socialize the educational system as those programs propose, the result would only substantiate the fears that many anxious people feel about socialist reform. Few people recognize that the implementation of socialist party programs for education would result in pure pedagogical madness. Although that may sound somewhat radical (and I apologize for that), I am interested only in developing an objective, practical idea. I am certainly not interested in working in any way toward any party-like program.

These introductory remarks raise the question about our current educational system: Where can we see the results of that educational system in ordinary life—that modern, practical life, from which there are universal calls for reformation?

If our interest in education is more than just theoretical, if, with our heart and soul, we are interested in the school system as the most important factor in human development, we must acknowledge that people who have no real insight into the needs and possibilities of life sometimes establish educational programs in a dubious way. Some people believe that those who want to reform life are capable of only the worst changes. We must ask those with such beliefs whether or not the souls of those they fear so much were educated in today's schools.

We look with fear at the proletariat today, and we have to admit that our anxiety is justified. If we are not too short-sighted, however, we have to admit that the proletariat went through our schools and that those schools produced the proletariat. The desires of the proletariat and also the errors in those desires should certainly help us understand the expression: "By their fruits you shall know them." I'm not trying to be superficially argumentative, but I want to point out the historical and cultural problem inherent in the modern educational system.

We need to be clear that, during the last three or four centuries—in particular the nineteenth century—a new kind of human being has arisen as the proletariat, a type of human being whose physical, soul, and spiritual makeup did not exist in earlier times. In contrast to other members of human society, the essence of modern members of the proletariat is that, to a much greater extent than before, their whole existence as human beings hangs in the air. From a pedagogical perspective, this is particularly interesting.

Concerning their own existence, individual members of the modern proletariat would have to say: If I lose my job, or am forced to give it up, I confront a void. They no longer feel connected with what binds human society. In that regard, we must also say that, while the proletariat developed, school education was incapable of developing a complete human being. It is certainly not the fault of the teachers. That fault lies with the schools' dependence on the state and economic forces. During the time just preceding our own, the growing child could have been worked with out of a genuine understanding of human development. But teachers were caught between two forces, which were not always compatible with the teachers' own view of how to educate children.

Today, in progressive schools that developed out of earlier times, teachers are caught between the parents and the state. Of course, there are always exceptions, and no single word completely describes all cases or any individual case. In general, however, we can say that modern teachers are presented with spoiled children in the classroom, and when they graduate them from school, the state immediately sucks out exactly what the teachers tried to give to the souls of those children.

Teachers today are caught between these two extremes, which are incompatible with what really needs to happen in schools. If teachers are really aware of their profession, then they can only groan under the burden of these two distortions of the children they teach—distortions caused by the parents and by the state. Of course, that is an extreme description of the problem. But do we ever receive any children from the parents other than those the parents themselves have raised? Children are brought up by the parents with all of their own prejudices. They are colored by all that parents carry in their attitudes and souls. Children are the product of their class and situation. On the other side, when we graduate children from school, we turn them loose into human life, sending them into a state-controlled society. The meaning of this is clear, particularly now, when humanity finds itself in such a terrible situation.

We have experienced major misfortune, and we will experience even more. Haven't we seen something in our misfortune that we might have seen in better times, if our insight had been sufficient? Haven't we seen that the essential characteristic of modern people is that inner strength of the soul was not developed during childhood—an inner strength of the soul that could help them move into life without life's destiny breaking their thinking, feeling, and willing?

People do not realize the extent to which broken people—broken human beings—exist in every social class. We see it in the dark, vague thoughts and ideas that modern people throughout the civilized world have about the terrible events that have befallen us. Is it possible for anyone to imagine how this occurred? Is it still possible for anyone to understand life? Is there anyone who still feels strong enough to take a truly active role in life? We don't realize how much our contemporaries are really broken human beings. We need to ask why our schools have not been effective in giving human beings what is needed to firmly grasp life so that they are not broken by life and destiny.

If schools had been allowed to spend more time teaching children what they need for a firm foundation in life, the situation today would be much different. However, that did not happen. Schools could have given people something, but those who are privileged and belong to the leading, upper classes of society do not place people in life according to their accomplishments in school, but according to family, relationships, protectionism, and similar things. They make sure that young people move into one or another position according to their connections. The only exceptions to this are those of the proletariat. Consequently, the proletarian is the real "modern" human being for the school.

Proletarian children cannot be spoiled as much by the parents. Other things could do that, but not the parents, because they don't have the time for them. When proletariat children leave school, they do not enter human society through family connections, protectionism, and so on, but must enter life through what is contained within their own souls. The proletariat—those who are let loose into human society and depend only on themselves—is, therefore, in a very different situation than people of higher social classes. It is this that has given our schools their particular flavor, and we must now give this some consideration. That is also why teachers need to work on our current major social problems.

The question of how we should shape human beings for life is being asked in very new ways. How can we teach in such a way that children develop their inner forces while attending school? How can we teach in a way that develops their forces of thinking, feeling, willing—making these forces strong enough in later life, so that life's destiny cannot break them? These questions arise with new urgency when we consider the proletariat. How should we raise children? How should we teach them in school? Such questions have assumed new meaning. That is why teachers must decide how children must develop in school in order to enter life.

Various party programs and opinions give us only a rather vague idea of what we now need. We see that modern people consider such questions by looking particularly at the school programs and ideas that socialists present. We only need to look at a few main points of those socialist ideas and programs for schools. Some socialist leaders emphasize, for example, the unified school, which should not be uniform; there should be as much differentiation as possible, in order to consider individual human capacities and interests. Socialists demand this by stating their desire for a differentiated curriculum in the unified school, but a unity in the organization. They mean that the unified school should be organized uniformly. The organizational form of the school should, therefore, not consider human individuality. Well then, how should we introduce that aspect?

It is very odd that such a school program can come from socialist groups at all, simply because socialists, with their materialistic understanding of history, always stress that the human being is completely the product of external conditions. They always emphasize that the human being is not at all influenced by moral, ethical, aesthetic, or religious concepts.

Socialism in its Marxist papacy calls all of that—ethical, moral, religious, and aesthetic views—merely an "ideological superstructure." Socialists view reality as an organization of economic relationships. They see the human being in the same way; everything else in the human soul dissolves into an ideological superstructure. Thus, socialism presents a school program that demands uniformity in organization and specialization in the curriculum. The curriculum would then bring what is, from their perspective, a more or less ideological superstructure. The organization would provide a situation in which to place the child to be formed into a human being.

When socialists demand such uniformity of organization, what they are really demanding, according to the basic ideas of socialism, is uniformity in all of human nature, since any differentiation within the curriculum results only in the object of that differentiation being merely an "ideological superstructure." Such a program demonstrates the contradictions that worm their way into current demands and the real results of such contradictions.

But, as for the demands themselves, can we do anything to discourage them? There is really nothing we can do about them. They are there. Humanity, at its present stage of development, has reached a certain level of awareness, a certain attitude in the soul expressed by such proletarian demands. Those demands are merely a signal that we must renew education in a way that is very different than how the proletariat imagines it. Through continuous development, a certain inner impulse has overtaken humankind, and that impulse has long been expressed in two words; but those words have become mere clichés, only slogans. Those words are *democracy* and *socialism.* These words arise with increasing strength from the foundations of human development. Now, although many foolish things are said about democracy and socialism, we must nevertheless admit that both are rising with increasing strength from human foundations. There are increased demands for state democratization and economic socialization. There is nothing we can do about those demands, since they are essential demands arising from the development of humankind. It is our task to take a reasonable position.

Just what do demands for democracy and socialism indicate? They mean that, more than ever before, the individual human will must guide all activity of state and economy. Through democracy, individuals—and this includes the subjugated proletariat—seek greater participation in state affairs than ever before. Through socialization, people hope for a more individual, a more personal, broader influence on the economy. We only need to recall how it was in earlier times, and we can easily see that human society was much more cohesive then. Individuals had a greater tendency to bow to tradition, necessity, and precedent. They tended to bow to the demands of those in higher positions or other authorities. Now, people want to be freed from subjugation to authority through democracy and socialism.

In regard to those specific socialist demands, what does society really require of schools? It requires the socialization of the school. People think that what occurs between adults in the realm of legal rights and economics should—perhaps in a milder form—also occur in the schools.

A proposal written by a socialist theoretician also says that we should eliminate things in the future. These days, everyone wants to eliminate things. This is what concerns people. The creation of something new is less interesting. Socialists want to eliminate the school principal's authority. To a certain extent, they also want to limit the authority of the teacher, and there is even talk of student-administered schools, with teachers as colleagues. By removing the principal and the school board, they believe that children will become particularly well-suited to democracy and socialism. This means creating for children what actually arises as a human developmental necessity in adult social relationships. However, they have forgotten something, and this can be seen as a deficiency in modern psychologists.

A good psychologist—someone who understands the soul— would never think that just because we loosen the bonds between adults, we should do that for children as well. A good psychologist would say exactly the opposite—that if we must now loosen adult social bonds so that we have more democracy and socialism, then there must be an even greater demand that we raise children so that later they have a capacity for democracy and socialism. If, however, we raise children in a school where democracy and socialism define the organization, later in life they will most likely be unfit for democracy and socialism. I am convinced that good psychologists who are serious about socialism and democracy would say, concerning human development, that in the feelings of children there is even greater reason to sow seeds that democracy and socialism cannot remove later on.

This leads us to the basic questions of teaching methods, or matters of pedagogy, because pedagogy must have a new face in the future. Pedagogy will have to begin with a deep understanding of human nature itself. In the future, in order to teach children effectively we will have to study human nature much more deeply than is currently possible. Our natural sciences have had major triumphs in the last four centuries. Those familiar with its conscientious methods know what scientific direction and research have given humanity in the last four centuries. Nevertheless, we cannot gain an understanding of the human being through conventional science, particularly when conventional science is concerned with fulfilling its own ideals. We will never understand the human being through conventional science! Using concepts based on observing nature, we can never recognize in ourselves what places us above the rest of nature—we can never recognize the spirit and soul.

It is understandable, therefore, that in an age when science has reached a certain pinnacle, understanding of the human being continues to regress, especially in Western civilization. This is something Eastern civilization accuses us of strongly. Those who understand science as we have spoken of it today, know that the true nature of the human being disintegrates when examined scientifically. Not only does human nature slip through the fingers of conventional science, but scientific thinking and its picture of the world have taken over modern human consciousness. It lives in every newspaper editorial and is a controlling factor in groups interested in today's needs. It also illustrates a significant dilemma. I could give you many examples, but I will present only one.

There is currently an important scientist, Oskar Hertwig, who in his area of biology is very good, perhaps one of today's greatest and most important biologists.[1] Many years ago he wrote a book, *The Development of Organisms: A Refutation of the Darwinian Theory of Chance.* From a scientific perspective, this is a very beautiful and important book. This unfortunate man, however, got the idea that he should write a book about social issues, but that book is complete nonsense. It is pure rubbish! This is a typical example.

It is now possible to have a deep understanding of science and scientific methods, and know nothing at all about social and ethical questions, in which human beings are far above nature. Because pedagogical thinking in particular is gripped by scientific thinking, people no longer really see the becoming, developing human being. The developing human being will be the greatest pedagogical enigma in the future. I am very much aware that what I have to say will seem quite obvious to many, but these days we too seldom consider the obvious.

There is an expression, and like many expressions, it is correct when used properly and otherwise completely false. This expression is: "Nature makes no leaps." But nature makes leaps everywhere. When a green leaf becomes a colorful flower petal, nature makes a leap. When the colorful flower petal becomes the pistil, nature once again leaps. Nature makes nothing but leaps. When considered in sufficient depth, we see that it is the same in human life.

Young human beings have three clearly separate periods of life. The first includes early childhood until the change of teeth. The change in the human organism that accompanies the change of teeth is much greater than modern physiology realizes. The entire nature of the human being, as it develops from birth until the change of teeth, changes considerably in the spirit and soul realm and, to a lesser extent, in the physical body after the change of teeth. The second period of life begins with the change of teeth and continues until puberty. The third continues from puberty until the early twenties. A more exact study of the human being based on their inner characteristics will need to be a part of anthropology in the future and will form the basis of methods for a real education.

During the first period of life, there is an aspect of growth that overshadows everything else for the developing child—that is, the child as imitator. Children have a tendency to imitate whatever anyone does, including facial expressions, ways of holding things, and degrees of dexterity. This goes much farther than people recognize. The effects of one person on another are much deeper than people generally realize. If our actions are those of good human beings when we are with children, they assume our gestures, goodness, capacity to love, and good intentions. This is particularly true when they begin to learn language. Whatever is ensouled by the parents and others in the child's surroundings floods into that growing human

being. Children completely adjust to and become like their surroundings, because the principle of imitation is the controlling
factor in human nature until the change of teeth.

This can be observed in specific instances. Some parents, for
example, came to me and said that something terrible had happened to their child. The boy had stolen something. I told
them that maybe that event had a different meaning for the
child, that perhaps the child was not a thief. I asked how old
the child was and the parents said he was five. I then asked
what had actually happened. They said that the child had
opened a drawer and taken some money. The child bought
some candy and gave some of it to other children. I told the
parents that they should certainly not allow this to continue,
but that the child only repeated what he saw almost every day;
his mother would go to the drawer, take out some money and
buy something. The child was only imitating and did not do it
as something bad, but as something that was natural within the
principle of imitation.

Before the change of teeth, therefore, parents should not
think that preaching and making good rules will have a positive
effect on the child. Those things have no significance for a child
during this period of development; rules are simply noise to the
young child's ears. Furthermore, in everything they do, parents
must act in a way that the child may be allowed to imitate them.
That is the best guide for child rearing during this period.

When you consider the current situation a little, you discover that it is not at all extreme to say that schools receive very
few well-behaved children. The basic principle of doing nothing, saying nothing, even thinking nothing that would spoil
the imitating child is not yet widely recognized. What does this
principle of imitation mean? When we consider the principle
of imitation during the first years of the child's life, when we
understand that properly observing the principle of imitation

can solidify the soul forces, we can then create something in children that enables them to be genuinely independent human beings later. What we sow often blossoms much later in life. Those who were never surrounded by people to whom they could devote themselves through imitation, making everything they did a part of themselves, will be unprepared for democracy and never enjoy independence. We need to consider this connection with life.

As I have said, we need to be very clear that the flower and fruit of what we sow in human life often mature much later than people realize. What we sow through the proper principle of imitation during the first seven years of life imprints deeply in a child's soul and finally comes to fruition at the age of twenty, then for the rest of life. It is generally true that when children are not brought up to pray, they cannot bring blessing to others later in life. What children learn often transforms in later life into exactly the opposite; prayer transforms into blessing, and so on.

The time of primary importance for school comes next— the period between the change of teeth and puberty. During this time the growing human being has a different basic development principle. If you really study human beings, you will observe that this developmental principle is a feeling for authority. When you raise a child during that period without a feeling for authority, certain forces of thinking, feeling, and willing cannot be developed. These need to be developed in the growing human being between approximately the ages of six and fifteen, when children need to progress to viewing others in such a way that they can say: What that person says is true. Children, of course, do not say that, but they should have that sense. We can never learn to look for truth in life if we have not first looked for it in someone who is an authority for us. If we do not place children in a position where, as their teachers, we become their absolute authority, it will be impossible to develop certain capacities of human nature in them.

In this regard, a kind of sacred feeling for authority needs to be present in the school. If you think that something other than this sacred feeling for authority leads to an understanding of democracy and social responsibility, if you believe that a democratic school organization leads to that goal, then you are surely on the wrong track. If you want adults that have inner maturity when confronted with democratic and social life, then they must learn as children to look up to their teachers as authorities. This is of primary importance in the atmosphere of the school if we want to educate children in a way that meets the needs of our time.

When children between the ages of seven and fourteen develop so that they reach out to become the other person, so to speak, who is their authority, then they develop into the well-rounded human being they are meant to be. A well-rounded human being will develop only when we have a deep pedagogical understanding of the many things children need during that time. We can say that the most important thing, particularly for that period of development, is the child's connection with authority.

You may know the remark made by Jean Paul—that in the first three years of childhood we learn more about life from our nanny than we learn in three years at the university.[2] That is how things were during Jean Paul's life. This remark is certainly correct, and one cannot argue with it. You must also realize, however, that many things depend on a child's physiology. Children should be handled properly regarding memory. A child notices and remembers as much as necessary before the change of teeth. With the change of teeth, however, it becomes necessary to take the child's memory into consideration. It is important during that time that we do not overburden the memory—that we don't try to impress something onto the memory that falls out on its own.

Again, as a result of poor modern psychology, people would not believe how bad it is for a human being when the memory is so mistreated during the first period of life that they immediately forget what they are forced to remember. This is why we should, whenever possible, use repetition and similar means. Repetition should be the basis of education between the age of seven and fourteen or fifteen. Whenever possible, we should summarize in short sentences things previously presented in detail so that they can be remembered, so that children really retain certain things in a way similar to how Christ remembered the Lord's Prayer. They should repeat something again and again and thus make it a part of the soul life.

We should always remember that, during that period of the child's life, we should always consider the child's developing soul forces. During this time, we make many mistakes by giving more attention to the school subjects demanded by life and by the state than we do to the developing human being. Common, everyday things, such as reading and writing, lack the inner basis of, say, geometry and arithmetic. The fact that we have the language we have is not fundamentally connected with anything external or generic. The existence of written letters doesn't have much to do with relationships in the world, whereas the existence of a triangle is based on the fact of its three sides, and that the sum of its angles is 180 degrees. All conventions, such as reading and writing, are primarily useful for developing the intellect and, in particular, reasoning. For now, it would be too much to fully explain that statement in a way acceptable to a genuine psychologist, but those who consider life fully will certainly see the truth of that statement.

By comparison, everything that corresponds to general relationships in the world or appeals to human memory—such as history or geography—is more connected, oddly enough, with the feeling forces. It forms feeling. Everything we teach young children about art forms the will. We should teach individual subjects with an eye on the developing human being and always remember that we form thinking with one thing, feeling with another, and willing with yet another thing. The important thing is the developing human being, not any particular collection of knowledge.

When we use these principles, children learn something seldom learned these days. They learn many things today, such as geography, arithmetic, drawing, and so on, but I don't want to speak about them. Children should learn as I just described, but there is not enough being taught about *how* to learn. Life itself is the greatest teacher. We leave school properly only if we leave with the capacity to learn from life for the rest of our years. But this is impossible if, in school, we are merely filled with facts. It becomes possible only when we use school to develop in the human soul the forces of thinking, feeling, and willing. That's how we learn to learn from life.

If we want democracy and a socialized society, then we should not be so arrogant that we think we are able to determine or know everything. We must move beyond delusions of grandeur, beyond the belief that, once we reach twenty-one, we will be reasonable, self-sufficient adults, suited for election to parliament to speak as people of experience. Rather, we must be educated in inner human modesty, so we can recognize that we are not, even for a moment, complete as human beings. Instead, we continue to develop from birth until death. We must recognize that every day of life has a special value, that it is not without purpose that we must learn to live through our thirties right after we have just gone through our twenties. We need to learn that each new day and each new year offers continual revelation.

What I have just said must become a real fact of life through our efforts in schools. During the scientific age, these things could not be considered properly. Certain principles crept into schools. For example, something that, considered from a certain perspective, is appropriate, may be seen from a different viewpoint as questionable—for example, providing visual examples of everything. I always get a small chill up my spine when I enter a classroom and see a calculator, which allows children to "see" how numbers are added.[3] This can be done with arithmetic, but only to a small degree.

Exaggerating the idea of providing visual examples, we could say that it would be justified as a teaching method only if we could visually illustrate everything in the world. But, do you actually believe that everything in the world can be illustrated?[4] There are many things in the world we cannot see, such as feeling, volition, sympathy, aversion, and so on. There's no way to illustrate such things; teachers must present them to the student through a kind of "fluid medium," if I may use that expression, through the principle of authority. From the perspective of cultural history, that is very important.

Today, it's apparent that we really educate children too intellectually, especially in the West. We teach children what they need for life based on reason. The program based most on reason is Marxism, which is completely intellectual. The essential characteristic of Marxism is its structure, which comes only through the intellect. People really understand Marxism only when they realize that it is dictated entirely by the intellect and sharp—even overly sharp—though comfortable, reasoning. In any case, it is based on the intellect.

In human nature and in the human soul, various soul forces balance one another. If one force overdevelops, the others are left behind. If the intellectual forces are overdeveloped, emotions remain at a lower level. You would then be strong, but without feeling. You would be dry. We see, therefore, that, in our time of the intellect, the most chaotic emotions and the most terrible instincts arise as "historical demands." This is coming to us here in Europe from the East and beginning to overpower Central Europe—in other words, basic, instinctive demands that form intellectualism's counterpart. I hope people begin to consider these interconnections.

As an example, there are two truly principled bourgeois philosophers. One of them, Avenarius, is more of a natural scientist of the nineteenth century.[5] The other is Mach.[6] One lived in Zurich where he taught, the other in Vienna. Avenarius and Mach attained the highest level of conventional scientific mentality, and they turned that mentality into a philosophical teaching. Why? Because their principle was everything for them: to use, whenever possible, only what can be observed through the natural sciences toward human knowledge.

They were truly very upstanding, good citizens—highly principled, I can assure you. But the philosophies developed by Avenarius and Mach have become the philosophy of the Bolshevik state in Russia! The connection might seem inexplicable. Superficially, we might say that it is because many Bolsheviks studied in Zurich. That doesn't explain it, however, because philosophies do not please someone who lacks an inner connection with them. They are connected by what their purely scientifically observable thinking represents. This is so one-sided that, through a hidden aspect of human nature, it awakens emotions and basic instincts in Bolshevism. It is not mere chance; there is an inner principle behind it. No one should consider these ideas more than teachers, because such matters are a profound part of cultural teaching methods.

We need to ask how we should educate children. At present we cannot allow ourselves to simply rely on confused, formal teaching methodology. We must include cultural history when creating a healthy program. Consequently, we need to balance the principle of observation with something that forms volition. For example, we have tried to replace mere physical gymnastics, which considers only limb movement, with eurythmy, which is an ensouled human movement. There may be some objections to this, but it is certainly in line with what I just suggested. People will eventually see that it is a way of ensouling gymnastics as much as it is an art, and that it can help education do something important with the will.

Similarly, we must change many entrenched beliefs if we want a truly human education that allows people to grow properly into democracy and socialism. Otherwise, democracy and socialism will become a terrible plague for civilized people. Primarily, we must consider that, when people are educated, they must acquire the capacity to practice what democratic socialism requires. This is necessary, since people want a voice in legal matters and economics through various advisory committees, which are intended to replace the effects of capitalism with the reason of works committees, transportation committees, and economic committees. Democratic socialism should not be just one more demand, but should also represent a system of human rights and responsibilities.

This is the degree of thoughtfulness needed to approach such matters today. In particular, we should take what lies behind the demands for democracy and socialism seriously, and bring that into our teaching methods and education. If people are to develop genuine insight into the needs and capacities of others, if our society is to become truly social, then, through the principle of imitation and the principle of authority, they develop within themselves the capacity for love that brings genuine fraternity to life. Without a feeling for human fraternity, socialism is a paper knife. Things would go badly if teachers were not asked to help reform our society, since the wind that brings health to our times blows only from the direction of education.

I can easily believe that, during this transitional period, teachers in particular may have serious doubts about how to create a school that educates with the same goal as the Union for a Threefold Social Order. That union sees the impossibility of working in this direction as long as schools are dependent on and permeated by the state. Maybe socialists should also consider this a little, since, to a certain extent, they want to socialize everything under government control. The social class that preceded the socialists placed their schools under government control. Schools are now completely under the control of the state, and we can surely learn what state control is by looking at that situation. Under the current plea for socialization, those who are serious and see things from a cultural and historical perspective have to acknowledge the importance of freeing the school from the state. Thus, a basic principle of the Union for a Threefold Social Order is to work toward an independent school system, making it free of the state so that the state does not even inspect schools. The activity of self-administered schools should arise purely from cultural needs, and much can grow from that. I want to present an example, so you can better understand this comprehensive subject.

We differentiate today between elementary grades, high schools, and colleges. Teaching methodology is also taught in the colleges. Now people want to improve the status of pedagogy, but it is still taught as a secondary subject. Until now, someone would be appointed professor of philosophy and then had to teach pedagogy, also. Mostly, it was a burden and not done very willingly. But this must change. In the future, all of culture must connect with human life in general. If we are to fulfill the ideal I described, teachers will also have to be psychologists. Teachers will have to educate the growing child through a deep understanding of the human being and, therefore, know best what is pedagogically correct. In the future, universities will appoint school teachers to teach pedagogy. And after teachers have done that for awhile, they will return to their schools to teach children and to gain new experiences in order to teach pedagogy once again. That will be a genuine "academic republic" as Klopstock dreamed of it.[7] We will not be able to progress until we view matters as thoroughly and deeply. It is the destiny of our time to inform practical life about such things.

In order to do that, everything cultural must be independent. The worst thing that could happen would be if the state, through coercion, no longer pays what the teacher needs. The situation for teachers would then be very bad. Nevertheless, teachers are a part of the economic process, just like everyone else. Aside from being teachers, these people will also be members of the third aspect of the threefold social order (the economic aspect), and will receive salaries from that independent economic system. The threefold social order will have an independent economic body, just as it has an independent legal body that will democratically take care of legal matters. Similarly, it will also have an independent cultural realm. What today goes into the pockets of teachers indirectly through taxes will, in the future, come directly from the economic aspect of society. Apart from that, an independent culture will foster the appropriate atmosphere for schools and teaching.

A proper evaluation of various goods and services also belongs to a healthy society. There must be an evaluation of goods and services. A healthy society, however, cannot see what a teacher actually gives to the coming generation as something to be purchased. What the teacher extends to other human beings is a gift from the spiritual world. A healthy society must understand that teachers are the medium through which human capacities, or individual human characteristics, are brought out of their dark shadows where they exist as a part of human nature. It is simply conventional narrow-mindedness to believe in paying according to what is actually accomplished in the schools.

The economic portion of the healthy threefold social order has to provide the possibility for teachers to live as others do. In our thinking, we need to strictly separate the potential for earning a livelihood and our evaluation of teaching. There can be no democracy without this healthy impulse. Democracy that equalizes everything and doesn't know the value of things will destroy everything; and socialism that believes everything can be paid for will destroy life itself. It is not just a matter of listening to teachers when moving toward democracy and socialization, but the assessment of teaching must also arise from an understanding of a healthy society.

The purpose of the Union for a Threefold Social Order is to see that each of these areas of life becomes independent. Therefore, it wants to base everything on an appropriate, healthy foundation. Everything that until now formed a disorganized, chaotic whole—in other words, the economy, the culture, and the state—should each become independent: an independent culture, an independent, democratic state, and an independent social economy. Human beings thus become the unifying element of those three aspects. People participate in all three areas, so we need not fear the loss of unity.

Some people believe that the threefold social order we are working toward would, so to speak, split a horse into three parts. They don't have the right picture of our goal. We are not trying to divide the horse into three parts; we simply want people to stop saying that a horse is real only when standing on one leg. The healthy social organism stands on three healthy legs: an independent cultural realm to which education and schools belong; an independent realm of legal rights to which the democratic state belongs; and an independent economy that is social. If we want to socialize legal rights—and culture even more so—then we would not have socialism in culture or legal rights, much less in the economy. That would result in a uniform economic life that could clothe and feed people, while slowly draining anything that might develop independently (that is, the legal and cultural realms).

This is a serious matter for both elementary and cultural pedagogy. It is an essential and comprehensive question right now.

In this rather long lecture, I have attempted as much as possible to show what the impulse of the threefold social order really is, and, in particular, what it wants to free from bondage. I particularly wanted to show what it wants to achieve in freeing culture, schools, and education from the bonds that currently restrain them. I would be extremely pleased if the underlying ideas I have presented would find interest and attention among teachers and instructors.

CONCLUDING REMARKS

In the following lively discussion, someone objected that proletarian children had been spoiled by bad examples and were unfit as the "new human being." Someone presented the idea that it would be better to replace authority with the leadership and obedience that were part of current school goals. The teacher's personality determines education, regardless of political context. A new way of training teachers to be independent is needed, but today teachers need the authority of the state behind them. The state gave teachers authority and had not disturbed them further, and consequently we cannot dispense with the state.

First, I would like to answer your questions. The chairman's question about proletarian children was first.

Perhaps I sounded as though I would designate the proletariat as the "prototype of the new human being." I ask that you do not understand this to mean that the "new human being" would be some kind of angel. Whenever something new is discussed, people make the common error of assuming that "new" always means "better," especially when discussing further human development. The idea of the proletariat as the paragon of the "new human" is the primary error of cliché-ridden party programs. For them, new is always better. I have not declared the proletariat the prototype of a *better* human being. I intended to say only that the proletariat exemplifies human beings who have developed during the past period—during the past three or four centuries, particularly the nineteenth century.

When I said that bourgeois parents spoiled their children, I also said that proletarian children were spoiled. I ask that you remember what else I said—that proletarian children were not spoiled by their parents because the parents have no time for that. Modern proletarian children are usually more rowdy than bourgeois children. We can easily agree on that. What the chairman (who teaches proletarian children) experiences in that regard is not as terrible as he thinks, as I see it. It could be imagined that proletarian children are so rowdy precisely because they exemplify the new human being; but the reason really lies elsewhere.

The reason is not that those parents belong to a certain social class and, therefore, the child imitates certain class characteristics. To put it bluntly, those children are brought up on the street and left alone, and they imitate all kinds of things. In general, they are in a bad situation. They have grown up among a part of humanity where there is nothing particularly good to imitate. Those children have grown up among a broad segment of humanity, so they exist much as the proletariat exists later. They have been raised by life. In contrast, bourgeois children have been more or less confined in a hothouse. That is the difference. There is no question that proletarian children imitate all kinds of things and arrive at school with the results of that imitation, imitating things that are not very desirable.

I thought it was important to show how the proletarian child develops when confronted with new tasks. First, because the child has no specific class characteristics from the parents, and second, because the child does not enter life as a protégé of a father, mother, brother or sister, aunt, uncle, or others. The proletarian child must depend on what is developed in the soul.

We repeatedly hear the phrase of a man who was not exactly exemplary in his work: "Success comes to those who work hard." Such things, however, have become mere clichés. It's easy to say "Success comes to those who work hard" when speaking about a nephew or younger sibling. We need to look at these things objectively, and not just hear the words. We live far too much in slogans because we so seldom view matters objectively. I ask you to consider this. That is what I have to say about imitation.

Regarding authority, it is natural that proletarian children do not often bring much feeling for authority to school. This is precisely what we need to work for, however, in developing and strengthening teaching methods. We need to develop, particularly in proletarian children, a real feeling for authority.

Someone also mentioned that it doesn't matter whether the person charged with developing thinking, feeling, or willing in a child does so within or outside the structure of the state. In spite of the fact that this question came up twice, I really cannot understand it. The important thing is that we do not rob teachers of their strengths of personality by forcing them to work within the confines of government regulations. You need only consider what it would mean if what entered the child's head did not come out of the free work of the teacher, but instead arose through regulations, curricula, and goals determined by the state. Think of what it would mean if education did not fully develop children, but instead turned them into people required to serve the state in the proper way and at the proper place as the state deems fit.

There was also an objection—one that always arises whenever this question is discussed—that the concern and desire for education is not very great right now. Parents would be happy if they did not have to send their children to school. Someone even said that no one should send their children to school. What I said, though, was in no way related with the superficial question of whether or not we should send children to school.

In my book, *Towards Social Renewal,* I speak about the child's right to education and that, in the future, an educational subsidy will be required from the economy. I am not saying those who would rather send their children out into the field than to school will not perceive compulsory education as a burden. What I am saying is that, in a healthy society, the child has a right to education.

Now, you could say that if the child has that right, then the state will still exist as a legal institution. (I do not know why people beat up on the state so much today, as one speaker did.) Today my intention was to speak only about cultural institutions. Here, someone might make the objection: if we recognize the child's right to an education, then parents will send their children to school, and we could, therefore, retain compulsory schooling. However, that has nothing to do with putting culture on its own two feet, making it independent, and it also has nothing to do with what is done in schools or in terms of school administration. Recently, I said about the same question that if we had no compulsory school, but the right to education existed, we could even turn things around so that those parents who do not want to send their children to school would lose their rights regarding the child's education and would be replaced by a guardian. The children would then, of course, go to school. These secondary questions can be answered if, with good intent, we genuinely understand the main point, which is to understand that everything depends on a free and independent culture.

Someone brought up another problem—that is, when the state, or life in general, does not accept what the teacher as an authority has planted in the children. However, it is the possibility of that difference that demands the separation of the educational system from the state. To make it impossible for the state to reject what has been placed into the child's soul through authority in the school, we need to place the school and the educational system firmly on their own feet. If the state has no authority over the teacher, then when someone is later forced to do something, that person will not think of a former teacher as worthless now that the state says it needs something else. That person will think back and feel the heavy burden of fate that he or she cannot carry out what the authority of the teacher placed in their soul. If you think about this in detail, you can see that the solution to this dilemma already exists. Because this dilemma has been lying for so long on people's souls, the demand for an independent spiritual life—and in particular, an independent educational system—has arisen from observation of life. All such things (and several dilemmas have been mentioned) can occur only when the educational system is placed into something with a democratic basis—the realm of legal rights.

From my perspective, what Mrs. B. said about authority was so abstract and theoretical that I do not believe it could have any practical significance in real life. From what I said, no one could think that I would suggest that children should decide whether or not a teacher is an authority. Such things result from the atmosphere of life itself.

In connection with the question of who will become teachers in the future, for several reasons a selection will not simply happen by examination or by simply knowing certain things. Under certain circumstances, a person can acquire such knowledge in only a few hours. You can find it in various handbooks. It is important, however, to consider the personalities and essential talents of the teachers. Of course, I'm not implying that if you did not already have some knowledge of these things, you could easily learn them in a few hours. I mean that, if you had some prior knowledge of a subject, you can easily relearn it when you need it again. The important thing is to have a certain guarantee about how a teacher becomes a teacher—a guarantee that the person and the entire personality exist in human culture in such a way that the teacher effectively conveys authority to the students.

These are things we need to consider much more deeply and much more fundamentally than we do when people speak of "leadership" and "following" or "communal leadership of the school," and so on. I ask you to recall what I said about "school community." It is important that you hear things as I said them and do not translate them into an abstract program already created for yourself.

There is also much to say about the separation of church and state. Historically, there was for a long time no alternative to having the school depend in some way on the church. More recently, the state has done a good deed by freeing education from the church and placing it on its own feet. However, now we have a situation where the school depends on the state, and we need to improve that by returning the school to its own footing. We need to recognize that these things can be seen in a one-sided, argumentative way. I often hear remarks that are not quite objective when people speak about such things today. Nevertheless, we need to be clear that it is inappropriate to work toward standardizing human souls through future educational methods or school organization. We cannot rule that something is valid in all cases for the spirit and soul, and then require that it be taught to children. We must be able to place ourselves into the souls of those who think and feel differently. It is important that we do not become afraid when, for example, Catholic parents demand that their children receive instruction in Catholicism. We don't have to fear that when we stand firmly on our own foundation.

Similarly, we don't need to fear the worldview of another if we are enthusiastic and strong in our own. Such attitudes can develop in free spiritual competition, but certainly not through laws. It is harmful when a church becomes the church of state through laws, with all the advantages of state protection; but it is just as bad when the state persecutes a church. The state should not support or persecute any attitude of soul in any way. If you begin with such thoughts and think them through sufficiently, you will discover that it is indeed necessary to make culture and, in particular, education, free and independent.

What was said about the authority exercised by the teacher (that young people should free themselves of it and not retain it throughout life) was either obvious or something was misunderstood. It is obvious that one should not go through life with the teacher's authority in the background. Such authority could cause a person to ask within: What would it be like if I were a teacher? What the teacher placed in that person's soul as authority would become that individual's own authority. Nevertheless, we must look at such matters much more thoroughly and with greater depth, because the authority of the teacher can indeed remain throughout one's life.

I've said that what a teacher provides in education cannot really be paid for. Payment involves something very different. In education the relationship between the teacher and the student can be developed in such a way that the teacher can remain an authority throughout a person's entire life. I ask you if there could be anything more beautiful than when, as an older person—say sixty years old—you can look back at your youth and recall a teacher and say that such a person was a true authority for you. Is there anything more beautiful than being able to say you are grateful for that teacher's gifts to you and that, as a consequence, you became what you are today. People can retain that kind of authority, and it can live through a life-long gratitude toward a teacher. The psychology appropriate to the tasks of today must include such things.

Someone said that the state is necessary or that we could replace it with some sort of cultural senate or some such thing. What I actually said was that those who have not felt the compulsion of the state have not actually experienced it. You see, the reality is that it is now second nature for people to want to be teachers employed by the state. When that has become second nature, you are no longer aware that it is not really your free and independent self who teaches from the source of culture. Instead, you have become accustomed to the state and to presenting what the state offers for instruction. You think you are free; but that feeling of freedom, especially the way people now feel, is certainly no proof that you really are free.

I would like to mention a person, Woodrow Wilson, who is a great world teacher according to many people, and his book *Concerning Freedom,* where he gives a strange definition of freedom. He defines it in such an odd way that it could make you climb the walls. Wilson says, roughly, that we can call a mechanism free that has no boundaries and works in whatever way required. He also says that we could call a ship free when it moves in a certain way according to the same principle. However, this mechanical freedom is not what we are talking about. It is something we have to feel.

There was also a great deal of discussion about many things that I certainly didn't say. Particularly, the man who defended the state said several such things, but I didn't say anything at all about the present state. Those who understood me properly will recall what I said—that the goals of modern socialists threaten to bring one thing or another to pass, and, thus, what could occur is exactly what should not happen. Consequently, we must arrange things in a certain way.

Now, I certainly cannot go into things that others merely misconstrued from my words and then turned into an argument. There is, however, one thing I do wish to address: that also there needs to be an authority for teachers. I have not said anything about the authority that teachers need, but only that teachers should be an authority for the child. Whether or not there is an authority for teachers is a totally different question, and it can be answered by saying that, ultimately, life itself takes care of that. Look at how life really is. This is something we consider far too little today. When you look at the way life really is, you have to admit that people are different from one another. You will have to admit that, in the end, someone who could be an authority in any one of many ways will always find a higher authority. Thus, everyone will always find an authority above themselves in real life. Of course, we do not need to go to an extreme here. Someone can be an authority simply because that person is more capable in some things.

When I spoke of Klopstock's "Academic Republic" I did not mean that everyone could do as they wish. It is much closer to the truth that people will not just do what they want to do, but that they will do what is required by culture in order to make it as fruitful as possible. There will be a voluntary acquiesce to authority. In an independent culture we can certainly conceive of a constitution that isn't based on rigid laws and petrified governmental rulings, but one based rather on real, living relationships among those who participate in it. We must, of course, first replace "the law" with free, personal, and flexible human relationships that are, therefore, not bound by rigid laws, carved in stone for eternity.

It is important that we give culture the opportunity to live in a form that arises from the forces already existing within it, so that teachers are not in some way dependent on a bureaucrat. Teachers must depend in an upright, objective way that results from culture itself. They must depend on others directly involved in culture and who are just as active culturally as the teacher. This is important. You can see today that there is a kind of fear of an independent culture and that many feel much safer under the state's protection. That is exactly the problem—that so many people feel good under state protection. And state protection will become even more desirable to people in the future.

Over the last several centuries, the state gained power through earlier conquests and so on, and then individuals wanted to connect themselves with that power for their own protection. For awhile the Church did that. The Church wanted not only the living word that flowed from the spirit, which could affect and convince people, but it also wanted the police to provide a little extra help. Others followed, including the educational system. In regard to education, people preferred not to have what was brought from the spirit affect the child, but to have the state's mandate behind it. Then, there were the various economic classes and organizations and finally those corporations (in Germany, mostly those in heavy industry) who also wanted to have some of the state's power. Now we have the Social Democrats who want to take over the state for themselves. Thus, the power of the state became the reservoir for everything.

In the future, we need to make sure that state power is no longer the refuge of whoever wants power. We need to give the state a democratic basis. It is important that the state be on a firm foundation where every adult is treated equally. We will then be working with a state of rights. It is odd that today's people don't want to recognize that, even though a comprehension of such relationships nearly occurred within that sphere of rights when there was a Prussian minister of culture.[8] You find in his *Limits of the State* some hint of what the state should really be. If the state is to be democratic, however, then it may include only what relates one adult human being to another.

We should remove culture from the state, and also exclude the economy from the state, especially when it concerns economic experience, credit, and so on. That means that if someone seriously wants democracy, such a person cannot at the same time want socialism and culture to be included in the state. That person would have to admit that to achieve democracy, the only healthy thing is to separate culture and economic activities as free and independent. The fact that people have not realized this (which is certainly the case in Russia) results in the so-called dictatorship of the proletariat through the extremely undemocratic, even anti-democratic, goals of the modern economy.

I was confronted with this in a very crude way a few months ago in Basel. Following one of my lectures, someone who was apparently a Communist stood and said that, in order to secure a healthy future, Lenin must become ruler of the world. Such people call for socialization, but they haven't the slightest understanding of what social is. They do not understand that we must first socialize the ruling relationships. Socialization does not consist of making the ruling relationship a monarchy, of making socialism imperial. People think they want to socialize, but they have no desire whatsoever to begin by socializing the relationships in government. Instead, they want to make some economic "pope" ruler of the entire world. That is how people think.

These are the contradictions that arise today. For that reason, I hope you have a feeling that the things expressed in the threefold social order are based on something deeper. I did not come to the idea of the threefold order through random abstract principles or what people commonly accept as belief. There are certainly a number of things that seriously need proper foundations, but the impulse for a threefold social organism arose from genuine, serious observation of life and from the feeling of serious concern for the primary cultural tasks today. If you honestly want socialism and democracy, then you cannot merely want what people often call "social democracy," since, in that case, culture is not properly considered.

Above all, those who honestly want democracy and socialism need a genuinely free cultural life, not something arbitrary. The impulse for a threefold organization resulted from a recognition of reality and a feeling for the seriousness of contemporary relationships. We here in Central Europe should particularly appreciate the gravity of our time—a time when we have to acknowledge this as a question of life or death and the need to rethink and relearn many old things. We cannot simply attempt small changes in various institutions. What we need is a genuine rethinking, a transformation in our feeling, and fresh learning. Only in that way can we understand our time and really progress!

NOTES

LECTURE 1
Dornach, August 9, 1919

1. Rudolf Steiner spent the previous four months in Stuttgart where he
   founded the Association for the Threefold Social Organism on April
   22, 1919. The task of that association was to publicize the thoughts
   contained in Steiner's book *Towards Social Renewal* (Rudolf Steiner
   Press, 1977, GA 23), and to help bring about a renewal of social life.
   During those weeks and months Rudolf Steiner held numerous lectures for workers with the goal of helping to form workers' councils
   (see *Betriebsräte und Sozialisierung*, Workers' councils and socialization, GA 331) and for industrialists and the general public interested
   in the problems of society (see *Neugestaltung des sozialen Organismus*,
   Reorganization of the social organism, GA 330). At the same time, he
   was involved in intensive preparations for the forming of the school
   for the children of the workers of the Waldorf Astoria Company.

2. See *Die Ergänzung heutiger Wissenschaften durch Anthroposophie*, Sup-
   plementation of contemporary science through Anthroposophy, GA
   73.

3. The reference here is to Richard Wahle (1857-1935), who wrote an
   article entitled "Concerning the Mechanism of Spiritual Life."

4. Translators' note: See *The Karma of Vocation*, Anthroposophic Press,
   1984, Lecture 9, for a more in-depth discussion of the role of the
   machine in modern life.

5. *The Education of the Child in the Light of Anthroposophy*, Anthroposophic Press, 1981 (revised edition in preparation).

6. Anatoli Lunatscharsky (1875-1933) was the commissioner for public
   education in Russia following the October Revolution in 1917 and

afterward president of the Academy of Art in Moscow. According to Lunatscharsky, the human soul is only the intersection of particular spiritual and sensible forces within social life.

7. Translators' note: "Helot: 1) a member of the lowest social and economic class of ancient Sparta thought to represent the conquered original population and constituting a body of serfs who were attached to the land, could not be sold, could be freed only by the state, were obliged to pay fixed portions of produce to the ruling Spartans, and were required to serve in the armed forces; 2) a member of any group of people deprived of rights and privileges and often exploited: serf." *Webster's Third New International Dictionary*, 1966.

8. Rudolf Steiner speaks in more detail about the various kinds of Greek sculpture in his lecture of June 9, 1919, contained in "Spiritual Scientific Consideration of the Social and Pedagogical Questions," typed manuscript, GA 192.

9. See Engels's book *Die Entwicklung des Sozialismus von der Utopie zur Wissenschaft*, (The development of socialism from utopia to science) 1919. There he states, "The necessity of state action in society will become superfluous in one area after another and will thus decrease of its own accord. The administration of commodities and the planning of production processes will replace the governing of people."

10. Refer to Rudolf Steiner's lecture given on April 14, 1914, contained in *The Inner Nature of Man and Life Between Death and Rebirth*, Rudolf Steiner Press, 1994, GA 153.

11. Lujo Brentano (1844-1931) was the brother of Franz Brentano, whom Rudolf Steiner often mentioned. He was an economist and supporter of economic liberalism and academic socialism. He supported, in particular, the trade unions and free trade.

12. Rudolf Steiner wrote a critical commentary on this article which was published in the *Beiträge zur Rudolf Steiner gesamtausgabe*, Vol. 103, Michaelmas, 1989.

13. There are a number of references to mammonism in the Bible, particularly, Matthew 6:19-34 and Luke 16:9-13. Rudolf Steiner also mentions mammonism in connection with the concept of capital in his lecture of October 5, 1919, in *The Anthroposophic Newsheet*, Vol. 20, 1952.

LECTURE 2
Dornach, August 10, 1919

1. Rudolf Steiner, *The Riddles of Philosophy,* Anthroposophic Press, New York, 1973. See p. 64 ff.

2. Rabindranath Tagore, (1861-1941) Indian poet, philosopher, and teacher. Through his book, *Gitanjali* (Song offerings), an English edition in prose of a selection of his religious poetry, he became internationally known. In 1913, he received the Nobel Prize for Literature.

3. Raphael Santi (1483-1520) was, along with Michelangelo and Leonardo da Vinci, one of the most important painters of the Italian Renaissance. Refer to Rudolf Steiner's lecture "Raphael Mission im Lichte der Geisteswissenschaft" (Raphael in the light of spiritual science), given on March 11, 1913, in *Beiträge zur Rudolf Steiner Gesamtausgabe,* Vol. 82, Christmas, 1983.

4. Refer to "The History of Art," typewritten manuscript, GA 292.

5. Refer to *The Spirit of the Waldorf School,* Anthroposophic Press, 1995, GA 297.

6. Emil Molt (1876-1936), director of the Waldorf-Astoria Company in Stuttgart and founder of the Waldorf School in Stuttgart in 1919 for the children of his employees. He called upon Rudolf Steiner to form and direct the school. Refer to his autobiography, *Emil Molt and the Beginnings of the Waldorf Movement,* Floris Books, 1991.

7. Georg Christoph Lichtenberg (1742-1799) taught physics at the University of Göttingen and became popular through his satirical essays against mysticism and the sentimental fantasies of the "Sturm und Drang" period. The aphorism quoted is actually, "When a book and head collide and there is a hollow sound, is that always due to the book?"

LECTURE 3
Dornach, August 11, 1919

1. During the absolutist French period of the eighteenth century, the mercantilists attempted to achieve a general high standard of living through government direction of industry and trade. However, the physiocrats saw agriculture as the main source of production and enrichment.

2. Adam Smith (1723-1790), British philosopher and economist, is recognized as the founder of classical economics. He was the first to provide a complete presentation of the liberal economic theories of the eighteenth century in his main work, *An Inquiry into the Nature and Causes of the Wealth of Nations*, 1776.

3. Pierre Joseph Proudhon (1809-1865), French socialist and anarchist, wanted to replace the state through voluntary organization into groups and associations, and is recognized as the founder of the anarchy movement.

4. François Marie Charles Fourier (1772-1837), French social reformer, proposed a social system in which associations for agricultural production and industry maintain direct connections and thus eliminated intermediary trade.

5. The meeting and the lecture referred to here are unclear. However, the lecture may be the one held on June 2, 1919, to which Rudolf Steiner was invited by a group of socialist students. No stenogram of that lecture exists.

6. Translators' note: Public law concerns the relationships within government and those between governments and individuals.

LECTURE 4

Dornach, August 15, 1919

1. See Rudolf Steiner's *The Riddles of Philosophy*, Anthroposophic Press, 1973, GA 18; *The Riddle of Man*, Mercury Press, 1990, GA 20; and *The Course of My Life*, Anthroposophic Press, 1986, GA 28.

2. Hermann Bahr (1863-1934), Austrian writer. Rudolf Steiner was acquainted with Hermann Bahr "since he was a very young student" and attentively followed his life. Refer to Steiner's lecture on December 10, 1916, in *The Karma of Untruthfulness, Part I*, Anthroposophic Press, 1988, GA 173.

LECTURE 6

Dornach, August 17, 1919

1. Johann Wolfgang von Goethe, *The Metamorphosis of Plants*, Biodynamic Farming and Gardening Association, 1993.

2. Concerning the differences between East and West in discovering the goals of humanity, refer to Rudolf Steiner's lecture given on July 20, 1919, in *Geisteswissenshaftliche Behandlung sozialer und pädagogischer Fragen,* Spiritual science and social and educational questions, GA 192.

3. Translators' note: For a warm, personal account of Rabindranath Tagore and his world, see Paramahansa Yogananda's *Autobiography of a Yogi,* Chapter 29 (Self-Realization Fellowship, Los Angeles, 1973).

4. Refer to Rudolf Steiner's lectures in *Aus schicksaltragender Zeit* (Out of a fateful time), GA 64, and *Aus dem mitteleuropäischen Geistesleben* (Out of the spiritual life of Middle Europe), GA 65.

5. The reference is to the Goetheanum in Dornach, designed by Rudolf Sreiner and built during the years 1913-1919. On New Year's Eve, 1922-23, the building was destroyed by fire. Later, a new structure on the same site was based upon a model designed by Rudolf Steiner. This second Goetheanum was completed in 1928. Refer to Rudolf Steiner's lectures in *Ways to a New Style in Architecture,* Anthroposophic Press, 1927, GA 286, and *The Building in Dornach,* typewritten manuscript, GA 287.

PART II: BACKGROUNDS OF WALDORF EDUCATION

PROLETARIAN DEMANDS
Stuttgart, April 23, 1919

1. This refers to the 1918–1919 German Revolution that abolished both the monarchy and the Soviet-style workers' councils and created a constitutional republic, the Weimar Republic.

2. This refers to the "Call to the German People and the Civilized World," an appeal that was signed by many well-known Germans and Swiss. An English translation is contained in *Towards Social Renewal* (Rudolf Steiner Press, London, 1977). Dr. Steiner refers several times in this lecture to a meeting of the signers of the "Call," which took place the previous day.

3. The length of the work day was then defined by the amount of materials available for production or the number of orders for products. People worked until either materials ran out or the orders were filled. This resulted in exhausting, long hours or impoverishing, short workdays.

4. *Surplus value* is the customary English Marxist translation of *Mehrwert*, which may be more accurately conceptualized as "increased value," which doesn't imply "unnecessary" or "extra." The common Marxist term is what an English-speaking audience might have heard.

5. Walther Rathenau (1867–1922), industrialist, statesman, and philosopher. His father established the General Electric Company in Stuttgart based on European rights to Thomas Edison's patents. Following the 1918 German Revolution, he began the middle-class Democratic party, positioned between the Social Democrats and conservatives. He supported the idea of industrial self-government, with employee participation and effective state control, rather than the universal nationalization supported by the Social Democrats. He became Minister of Reparations in 1921 and later Minister of Foreign Affairs. He was assassinated in June 1922.

THE SOCIAL BASIS OF PUBLIC EDUCATION
LECTURE 1, *Stuttgart, May 11, 1919*

1. Rudolf Steiner Press, 1977.

2. Oskar Hertwig, 1849-1922, author of *Das Werden der Organismen, Eine Widerlegung der Darwinschen Zufallslehre* (The development of organisms, a refutation of Darwin's theory), 1916 and *Zur Abwehr des ethischen, des sozialen und des politischen Darwinismus* (On the defense of ethical, social, and political Darwinism), 1918.

3. *Der Leuchter, Weltanschauung und Lebensgestaltung,* published in Darmstadt, 1919. The cited text is from Jakob von Uexküll (1864-1944). It is contained in his essay, "Der Organismus als Staat und der Staat als Organismus" (The organism as a state and the state as an organism). In his essay, "Der Aufstieg der Seele" (The development of the soul), Friedrich Niebergall says, "As enticing as it might be to speak in this connection about Johannes Müller and his 'direct, personal, original life and the creation of living processes at the center of the eye,' we still want to turn to another philosophical area of spiritual life." There follows a short section about Rudolf Euken and then later a longer section about the "Theosophy that at present is connected primarily with the name of Rudolf Steiner."

4. The original stenographer's report contained the word "geography" here, which has been replaced with "geometry" in the most recent German edition.

5. Translators' note: In the context of the relationship of eurythmy to physical education, other translators have often rendered the word "add" as "replace" (the German text is ambiguous). However, in answer to a question posed at the end of his lecture to public school teachers in Basel, November 17, 1919, in *Spirit of the Waldorf School* (Anthroposophic Press, 1995) Steiner clarified this point:

> Perhaps I did not make this clear enough in the lecture.... I need to mention this so as not to leave the impression that I believe we should drop gymnastics.
>
> You see, in the Waldorf School in Stuttgart, we have a period of normal gymnastics and a period of eurythmy, consisting of more than you see in an artistic presentation. Thus, we take into account the requirements that you justifiably presented.
>
> What is important to me is that along with the physical, the physiological that forms the basis of gymnastics, we add the spirit and soul, so that both things are present. Just as people themselves consist of a totality in the interaction of body, soul, and spirit, what is truly the soul, recognizable for itself, also works in the movements that people carry out in gymnastics and such. We are not at all concerned with eliminating gymnastics. Quite the opposite. It is my desire that gymnastics be enriched with eurythmy. We should not eliminate one single exercise on the parallel bars or high bar. We should leave out nothing in gymnastics. However, what eurythmy attempts is that instead of asking how we can handle this or that muscle form the physiological point of view, the question becomes, How does a soul impulse work? In other words, alongside what already exists, we add something else.

See also Lecture 13, September 4, 1919, in *The Foundations of Human Experience*, Anthroposophic Press, 1996, where Steiner says, "The more we alternate physical education with eurythmy, the more we can bring the need for sleep and wakefulness into harmony."

6. Emil Molt, 1876-1936, Director of the Waldorf-Astoria Cigarette Factory, created for the workers of his factory a school for continuing education. It was his desire to have a school for his workers' children

patterned after Rudolf Steiner's descriptions. This became the impulse for the founding of the first Waldorf School in Stuttgart.

7. Ulrich von Wilamowitz-Möllendorff, 1848-1931, Professor of Classics in Göttingen and Berlin. Among his numerous publications about Greek poets and philosophers, he published translations of the Greek tragedies in 1899-1924.

8. Translators' note: Rudolf Steiner describes his work with this child in detail in Chapter 6 of *The Course of My Life*, Anthroposophic Press 1986, GA 28

9. Translators' note: From the 1963 Encyclopedia Britannica,

> Pluralism and monism are theories giving respectively the answers "many" and "one" to two quite distinct questions: first, *how many things are there in the world?*; and second, *how many kinds of things are there in the world?* Much confusion is engendered if this distinction is not clearly maintained. Pluralism and monism as theories of substance, answers to the first question, have no necessary connection with pluralism and monism as theories of *kinds* of substance, answers to the second question. Philosophers can be cited to exemplify the four possible combinations of views: Descartes is a pluralist and Hegel a monist in both senses, Spinoza is a monist of substance and a pluralist of kinds, Bertrand Russell a pluralist of substance and a monist of kinds. Such definitions as "monism attempts to explain the entire universe from a single principle" misleadingly suggest, by compounding the two questions, that Spinoza and Russell are guilty of some inconsistency from which the writings of Descartes and Hegel are free.
>
> A theory of substance seeks to establish the nature of what it is that can properly be said to exist independently or in its own right, or, again, what are the ultimate subjects of discourse.... A theory of kinds, "ultimate" kinds, of substance seeks to establish how many irreducibly different kinds of knowledge or experience we must admit.... Whether or not parts of the world are independent of one another and whether or not there is more than one source of knowledge are questions whose internal connection, if any, does not at once leap to the eye. Hence the importance of distinguishing the varieties of pluralism and monism to which the attempt to answer them gives rise.

10. Rudolf Eucken, 1846-1926, *Der Kampf um einen geistigen Lebensinhalt* (The struggle for a spiritual content of life), 1896, and

Einführung in eine Philosophie des Geisteslebens (Introduction to a philosophy of the spiritual life), 1908.

11. Friedrich Paulsen, 1846-1908, *Einleitung in die Philosophie* (Introduction to philosophy), 1892, and *Systems der Ethik* (Ethical systems), 1889.

LECTURE 2, *Stuttgart, May 18,1919*

1. Wilhelm Förster, 1832-1921.

2. Refer to Rudolf Steiner's lecture on May 16, 1919, "Einzelheiten über die Neugestaltung des sozialen Organismus" (Details on the reorganization of the social organism), in *Neugestaltung des socialen Organismus* (Reorganization of the social organism), GA 330.

3. The Deutsche Bank, which had already financed the construction of the railway connection between Constantinople and Ankara, received the concession for the extension of the railway through Baghdad to Basara on the Persian Gulf in 1903. In the following year, this led to a political discussion with England and Russia, who feared a broadening of German influence in this area.

4. Karl Helfferich, 1872-1924, became Director of the Baghdad Railway in 1906 and of the Deutsche Bank in 1908. In the years 1915-1917, in his positions as Secretary of the Treasury and then Secretary of the Ministry of Internal Affairs, he was responsible for financing the war and for German financial policy during the war. On April 23, 1924, he died in a railway accident near Bellinzona shortly before a major electoral victory of his party.

5. Wolfgang Kapp, 1858-1922, Governor of East Prussia 1906-1920 and cofounder of a German nationalist political party (Vatterlandspartei).

6. Theobald von Bethmann Hollweg, 1856-1921, German Chancellor from 1909-1917. On June 5, 1916, Hollweg gave a speech in the Reichstag, "Gegen Schmähschriften des Generallandschaftsdirektors Kapp," (Concerning Governor Kapp's derogatory remarks).

7. Rabindranath Tagore, 1861-1941, Indian poet and religious philosopher.

8. Herman Grimm, 1828-1901. His statement is contained in his book *Fünfzehn Essays Vierte Folge Aus den letzten fünf Jahren* (Fifteen essays, part 4 from the last five years).

LECTURE 3. *Stuttgart, June 1, 1919*

1. Rudolf Steiner describes his work with this child in detail in Chapter 6 of *The Course of My Life*, Anthroposophic Press, 1986, GA 28.

2. Refer to Rudolf Steiner's lecture on May 31, 1919, in *The Threefold Order of the Body Social*, typed manuscript, Anthroposophical Society of Great Britain, GA 330.

3. *Towards Social Renewal*, Rudolf Steiner Press 1977.

4. Translators' note: Rudolf Steiner's position regarding ownership and disposition of capital (both the means of production and investment capital), as expressed in *Towards Social Renewal*, is much more complex and differently directed than this one sentence of a brief lecture would imply. In sum, private ownership and management of capital and of the means of production is retained, but the right of disposition of such capital (e.g., the right to transfer ownership, to use or not use a given means of production, to designate successive management) is regulated and administered by the rights realm (i.e., the government) such that individual contributions would be fairly compensated while an optimal benefit for society as a whole would be safeguarded. The goal is that the means of production always be in the hands of those best qualified to manage them and that unjustified acquisition of power be disallowed. While some of his presentation contains self-contradictory elements insofar as the specifics of administering the disposition of capital is concerned (he was giving examples, not proposing a formula), the thrust of Steiner's explanation is that at any given instance, those responsible within the rights realm would do whatever was necessary to effect a balance between the needs of the economy and those of the other realms, and to create the social foundation for a consistently optimal level of economic productivity. Refer to *Towards Social Renewal*, Chapter 3, "Capitalism and Social Ideas (Capital, Human Labor)."

5. Translators' note: The manner of Steiner's presentation here could easily lead anyone encountering this idea for the first time to conclude that Steiner believed that all humanity need do is to improve the relationship of people to the means of production and then all goodness will automatically flow into the world. The reverse is closer to the case. In his lecture of February 12, 1921, in *Wie Wirkt Man für den Impuls der Dreigliederung des Socialen Organismus?* (How does one work for the impulse of threefoldness of the social organism?), GA

338, available in a typed manuscript, *Anthroposophy and the Threefold Social Order*, he says:

> ... That people today are in a greater state of distress than they were before has not been caused by physical occurrences, but rather by the spirit of the people. When people today are in distress, this has been caused by false spirituality, by false thinking. Thus, there can be no other solution to bring people out of this predicament than that right thinking replace false thinking. The effects of nature or some unknown powers have not brought people into the present situation, rather people themselves have caused it. If there is need, then it is people themselves who have caused this need; if people have nothing to eat, then it is people themselves who have been closed to receiving food. Everything depends upon the fact that we may not begin from the false assumption that some unknown powers have caused this present emergency, and that we must first solve these present problems before we can begin to work on the right way of thinking. Rather, everything depends upon the fact that we must make it clear that the false thinking of humanity has caused this emergency, so that only right thinking can cause the solution to this emergency.
>
> We must keep in mind the various aspects of the superstition that we must first provide bread for humanity, and then, when they have enough to eat, they will find a better way of thinking. This is a terrible superstition. We will achieve no prosperity in today's civilization if we do not decide to put this superstition aside and replace it with the right belief that a reversal, a renewal, of thoughts about the world must occur. This is what must happen in a large enough number of people.

6. Translators' note: The Spartacus League was the far-left-wing of the German Social Democratic Party and was led by Rosa Luxemburg. Its main difference with the rest of the party was that it believed that any path of compromise or moderation led away from the goal of achieving a new socialist society. Ultimately, it broke with the Social Democrats and joined the German Communist Party. The Bolsheviks held a similar position within the International Communist Party. Under Vladimir Lenin, they ultimately led the communist revolution that ended Czarism in Russia.

7. Translators' note: There is a similar, oft-quoted passage from Rudolf Steiner's essay "Anthroposophy and the Social Question" (*Lucifer-Gnosis* October, 1905, GA 34), Mercury Press, 1982:

> In a community of human beings working together, the well-being of the community will be greater, the less the individual claims for himself the proceeds of the work he has himself done, i.e., the more of these proceeds he makes over to his fellow workers, the more his own requirements are satisfied, not out of his own work done, but out of work done by the others.

This passage has often been interpreted to mean ethical altruism. In Lecture 3, July 26, 1922, in *World Economy*, Rudolf Steiner Press, 1977, pp. 40-43, Steiner makes it clear that he was referring to something else, namely, the economic fact of the division of labor in modern society and economics, and that this fact exists objectively, independent of ethical altruism.

> ... simultaneously with this culmination of the emancipated life of Rights and human Labor, another element arises which— though it undoubtedly existed in former epochs of human evolution— had quite a different significance in those times owing to the operation of religious impulses.... I refer to the Division of Labour.
>
> ... You see, in former epochs the division of labour had no peculiar significance. It too was embraced in the religious impulses. Everyone, so to speak, had his proper place assigned to him. But it was very different when the democratic tendency united with the tendency to division of labor—a process which only began in the last few centuries and reached its climax in the nineteenth century. Then the division of labour gained very great significance.
>
> ... For the division of labor entails a certain economic consequence ... if we think it abstractly to its conclusion, we must say that in the last resort it leads to this: No one uses for himself what he produces....
>
> ... you will realize that the division of labour tends towards this conclusion: No one any longer works for himself at all. All that he produces by his labour is passed on to other men,

and what he himself requires must come to him in turn from the community....

... the more the division of labour advances, the more it will come about that one man always works for the rest—for the community in general—and never for himself. In other words, with the rise of the modern division of labour, the economic life as such depends on Egoism being extirpated, root and branch. I beg you to take this remark not in an ethical but in a purely economic sense. Economically speaking, egoism is impossible. I can no longer do anything for myself; the more the division of labour advances, the more must I do everything for others.

... The summons to altruism has, in fact, come far more quickly through purely outward circumstances in the economic sphere than it has been answered on the ethical and religious side....

Human thought on Ethics was far from having arrived at a full appreciation of altruism at a time when the division of labour had already brought about its appreciation in the economic life. Taking it, therefore, in its purely economic aspect, we see at once the further consequences of this demand for altruism. We must find our way into the true process of modern economic life, wherein no man has to provide for himself, but only for his fellowmen. We must realize how by this means each individual will, in fact, be provided for in the best possible way.

.... In this lecture I am speaking neither idealistically nor ethically, but from an economic point of view. What I have just said is intended in a purely economic sense. It is neither a God, nor a moral law, nor an instinct that calls for altruism in modern economic life—altruism in work, altruism in the production of goods. It is the modern division of labour—a purely economic category—that requires it.

... This is approximately what I desired to set forth in the essay I published long ago ["Anthroposophy and the Social Question"].

THE TASKS OF SCHOOLS
Stuttgart, June 19, 1919

1. Oskar Wilhelm Hertwig (1849–1922), embryologist and professor at Jena and Berlin. Demonstrated fertilization to be the fusion of the nuclei of sperm and ovum; he and his brother Richard artificially fertilized sea urchin's egg.

2. Jean Paul Friedrich Richter (1763–1825), generally known as *Jean Paul*; his romantic novels include *Hesperus* and *Titan*; his book on pedagogy was *Vorschule der Ästhetik* ("Reflections on art"); he also wrote on politics.

3. This refers to mechanical nature of "adding machines," which had, for example, ten columns of ten keys with a large lever on the side. The children could "see" each number keyed in, the lever pulled, and the next number entered the same way. The result appeared on a paper strip.

4. The first picture book for learning the words for things, *Orbis Sensualium Pictus* ("The Sense World in Pictures"), was written by Johann Comenius in 1658. It was translated into English and used as a textbook until the late 1700s. By mechanizing the process of learning addition with adding machines (or calculators) and reading through the use of picture books, the child's imagination and feeling for the process is bypassed.

5. Richard Avenarius (1843–1896), professor in Zurich; he advocated the principle of *empiriocriticism*, or the doctrine of undivided pure experience in relation to environment and knowledge.

6. Ernst Mach (1838–1916), physics professor in Prague and philosophy professor in Vienna. Researched physics, physiology, and psychology of the senses, especially in relation to theory of knowledge; he helped to establish empiriocriticism and the basic principles of modern scientific positivism. As a result of his study of projectiles, his name is related to the speed of sound.

7. Friedrich Klopstock (1724–1803), a poet whose success arose from the publication of the first three cantos of his religious epic *Der Messias.*

8. Wilhelm von Humboldt (1767–1835), philologist and diplomat, Prussian foreign minister and minister of education, established Humboldt University in Berlin.

FURTHER READING

Basic Works by Rudolf Steiner

Anthroposophical Leading Thoughts: Anthroposophy as a Path of Knowledge: The Michael Mystery, Rudolf Steiner Press, London, 1985.

Anthroposophy (A Fragment), Anthroposophic Press, Hudson, NY, 1996.

An Autobiography, Steinerbooks, Blauvelt, NY, 1977.

Christianity as Mystical Fact, Anthroposophic Press, Hudson, NY, 1997.

The Foundation Stone / The Life, Nature, and Cultivation of Anthroposophy, Rudolf Steiner Press, London, 1996.

How to Know Higher Worlds: A Modern Path of Initiation, Anthroposophic Press, Hudson, NY, 1994.

Intuitive Thinking as a Spiritual Path: A Philosophy of Freedom, Anthroposophic Press, Hudson, NY, 1995 (previously translated as *Philosophy of Spiritual Activity*).

An Outline of Occult Science, Anthroposophic Press, Hudson, NY, 1972.

A Road to Self-Knowledge and The Threshold of the Spiritual World, Rudolf Steiner Press, London, 1975.

Theosophy: An Introduction to the Spiritual Processes in Human Life and in the Cosmos, Anthroposophic Press, Hudson, NY, 1994.

THE FOUNDATIONS
OF WALDORF EDUCATION

THE FIRST FREE WALDORF SCHOOL opened its doors in Stuttgart, Germany, in September, 1919, under the auspices of Emil Molt, the Director of the Waldorf Astoria Cigarette Company and a student of Rudolf Steiner's spiritual science and particularly of Steiner's call for social renewal.

It was only the previous year—amid the social chaos following the end of World War I—that Emil Molt, responding to Steiner's prognosis that truly human change would not be possible unless a sufficient number of people received an education that developed the whole human being, decided to create a school for his workers' children. Conversations with the Minister of Education and with Rudolf Steiner, in early 1919, then led rapidly to the forming of the first school.

Since that time, more than six hundred schools have opened around the globe—from Italy, France, Portugal, Spain, Holland, Belgium, Great Britain, Norway, Finland, and Sweden to Russia, Georgia, Poland, Hungary, Romania, Israel, South Africa, Australia, Brazil, Chile, Peru, Argentina, Japan, and others—making the Waldorf school movement the largest independent school movement in the world. The United States, Canada, and Mexico alone now have more than 120 schools.

Although each Waldorf school is independent, and although there is a healthy oral tradition going back to the first Waldorf teachers and to Steiner himself, as well as a growing body of secondary literature, the true foundations of the Waldorf method and spirit remain the many lectures that Rudolf Steiner gave on the subject. For five years (1919–24), Rudolf Steiner, while simultaneously working on many other fronts, tirelessly dedicated himself to the dissemination of the idea of Waldorf education. He gave manifold lectures to teachers, parents, the general public, and even the children themselves. New schools were founded. The movement grew.

While many of Steiner's foundational lectures have been translated and published in the past, some have never appeared in English, and many have been virtually unobtainable for years. To remedy this situation and to establish a coherent basis for Waldorf education, Anthroposophic Press has decided to publish the complete series of Steiner lectures and writings on education in a uniform series. This series will thus constitute an authoritative foundation for work in educational renewal, for Waldorf teachers, parents, and educators generally.

RUDOLF STEINER'S LECTURES
(AND WRITINGS) ON EDUCATION

I. *Allgemeine Menschenkunde als Grundlage der Pädagogik. Pädagogischer Grundkurs,* 14 Lectures, Stuttgart, 1919 (GA 293). Previously *Study of Man. The Foundations of Human Experience* (Anthroposophic Press, 1996).

II. *Erziehungskunst Methodische-Didaktisches,* 14 Lectures, Stuttgart, 1919 (GA 294). *Practical Advice to Teachers* (Rudolf Steiner Press, 1988).

III. *Erziehungskunst,* 15 Discussions, Stuttgart, 1919 (GA 295). *Discussions with Teachers* (Anthroposophic Press, 1997).

IV. *Die Erziehungsfrage als soziale Frage,* 6 Lectures, Dornach, 1919 (GA 296). *Education As a Force for Social Change* (previously *Education as a Social Problem*) (Anthroposophic Press, 1997).

V. *Die Waldorf Schule und ihr Geist,* 6 Lectures, Stuttgart and Basel, 1919 (GA 297). *The Spirit of the Waldorf School* (Anthroposophic Press, 1995).

VI. *Rudolf Steiner in der Waldorfschule, Vorträge und Ansprachen,* Stuttgart, 1919–1924 (GA 298). *Rudolf Steiner in the Waldorf School—Lectures and Conversations* (Anthroposophic Press, 1996).

VII. *Geisteswissenschaftliche Sprachbetrachtungen,* 6 Lectures, Stuttgart, 1919 (GA 299). *The Genius of Language* (Anthroposophic Press, 1995).

VIII. *Konferenzen mit den Lehren der Freien Waldorfschule 1919–1924,* 3 Volumes (GA 300). *Conferences with Teachers* (Steiner Schools Fellowship, 1986, 1987, 1988, 1989).

IX. *Die Erneuerung der Pädagogisch-didaktischen Kunst durch Geisteswissenschaft,* 14 Lectures, Basel, 1920 (GA 301). *The Renewal of Education* (Kolisko Archive Publications for Steiner Schools Fellowship Publications, Michael Hall, Forest Row, East Sussex, UK, 1981).

X. *Menschenerkenntnis und Unterrichtsgestaltung,* 8 Lectures, Stuttgart, 1921 (GA 302). Previously *The Supplementary Course—Upper School* and *Waldorf Education for Adolescence. Education for Adolescents* (Anthroposophic Press, 1996).

XI. *Erziehung und Unterricht aus Menschenerkenntnis,* 9 Lectures, Stuttgart, 1920, 1922, 1923 (GA 302a). The first four lectures available as *Balance in Teaching* (Mercury Press, 1982); last three lectures as *Deeper Insights into Education* (Anthroposophic Press, 1988).

XII. *Die Gesunder Entwicklung des Menschenwesens,* 16 Lectures, Dornach, 1921–22 (GA 303). *Soul Economy and Waldorf Education* (Anthroposophic Press, 1986).

XIII. *Erziehungs- und Unterrichtsmethoden auf Anthroposophischer Grundlage,* 9 Public Lectures, various cities, 1921–22 (GA 304). *Waldorf Education and Anthroposophy 1* (Anthroposophic Press, 1995).

XIV. *Anthroposophische Menschenkunde und Pädagogik,* 9 Public Lectures, various cities, 1923–24 (GA 304a). **Waldorf Education and Anthroposophy 2** (Anthroposophic Press, 1996).

XV. *Die geistig-seelischen Grundkräfte der Erziehungskunst,* 12 Lectures, 1 Special Lecture, Oxford 1922 (GA 305). **The Spiritual Ground of Education** (Garber Publications, 1989).

XVI. *Die pädagogisch Praxis vom Gesichtspunkte geisteswissenschaftlicher Menschenerkenntnis,* 8 Lectures, Dornach, 1923 (GA 306). **The Child's Changing Consciousness As the Basis of Pedagogical Practice** (Anthroposophic Press, 1996).

XVII. *Gegenwärtiges Geistesleben und Erziehung,* 4 Lectures, Ilkeley, 1923 (GA 307). **A Modern Art of Education** (Rudolf Steiner Press, 1981) and **Education and Modern Spiritual Life** (Garber Publications, n.d.).

XVIII. *Die Methodik des Lehrens und die Lebensbedingungen des Erziehens,* 5 Lectures, Stuttgart, 1924 (GA 308). **The Essentials of Education** (Anthroposophic Press, 1997).

XIX. *Anthroposophische Pädagogik und ihre Voraussetzungen,* 5 Lectures, Bern, 1924 (GA 309). **The Roots of Education** (Anthroposophic Press, 1997).

XX. *Der pädagogische Wert der Menschenerkenntnis und der Kulturwert der Pädagogik,* 10 Public Lectures, Arnheim, 1924 (GA 310). **Human Values in Education** (Rudolf Steiner Press, 1971).

XXI. *Die Kunst des Erziehens aus dem Erfassen der Menschenwesenheit,* 7 Lectures, Torquay, 1924 (GA 311). **The Kingdom of Childhood** (Anthroposophic Press, 1995).

XXII. *Geisteswissenschaftliche Impulse zur Entwicklung der Physik. Erster naturwissenschaftliche Kurs: Licht, Farbe, Ton—Masse, Elektrizität, Magnetismus,* 10 Lectures, Stuttgart, 1919–20 (GA 320). **The Light Course** (Steiner Schools Fellowship,1977).

XXIII. *Geisteswissenschaftliche Impulse zur Entwicklung der Physik. Zweiter naturwissenschaftliche Kurs: die Wärme auf der Grenze positiver und negativer Materialität,* 14 Lectures, Stuttgart, 1920 (GA 321). **The Warmth Course** (Mercury Press, 1988).

XXIV. *Das Verhältnis der verschiedenen naturwissenschaftlichen Gebiete zur Astronomie. Dritter naturwissenschaftliche Kurs: Himmelskunde in Beziehung zum Menschen und zur Menschenkunde,* 18 Lectures, Stuttgart, 1921 (GA 323). Available in typescript only as **"The Relation of the Diverse Branches of Natural Science to Astronomy."**

XXV. **The Education of the Child and Early Lectures on Education** (A collection) (Anthroposophic Press, 1996).

XXVI. Miscellaneous.

INDEX

DURING THE LAST TWO DECADES of the nineteenth century the Austrian-born Rudolf Steiner (1861–1925) became a respected and well-published scientific, literary, and philosophical scholar, particularly known for his work on Goethe's scientific writings. After the turn of the century he began to develop his earlier philosophical principles into an approach to methodical research of psychological and spiritual phenomena.

His multifaceted genius has led to innovative and holistic approaches in medicine, philosophy, religion, education (Waldorf schools), special education, economics, agriculture (Biodynamic method), science, architecture, drama, the new arts of speech and eurythmy, and other fields of activity. In 1924 he founded the General Anthroposophical Society, which today has branches throughout the world.